PRAISE

"No matter where you are in life and in each of the Pillars, you can look within yourself and find more ways to apply each Pillar to your life. As you go through the Pillars, you will see the interplay between them. I enjoyed seeing how they worked together, and how exploring one deepened the others. This is a program, and a book, that you could redo at least once a year. Each time you will find new ideas to explore, you will find greater depths in yourself and your experiences. I have taken the program once, and am excited to read the book and explore more." ~Melody Owen

"Dynamic You™ has helped me face my fears; there is no greater gift than the gift of self belief and awareness." ~Sukeina Jethabhai

"I highly recommend Dynamic You™. It gives you a chance to work on you and gives you some specific tools to use for your personal development that will help you in business and life. Being a part of Dynamic You™ gave me that last little push I needed to start my new business." ~Cora Naylor

"The Dynamic You™ Program provided me with the ability to see myself as a valued member of my community, and realizing I am not the only one who has these situations. I gained valuable insight from having to:

1. Look at the situation.

2. Acknowledge habits

3. Action change by completing the challenges

4. Reflection and accountability

5. Growth was achieved by implementing the change

Through each of Diane's programs, I experience an increase in self-confidence, growth, and self-belief." ~Claire Madin

"Dynamic You™ is a great 6-week program where the focus was on me. It was tough for me to schedule time to take care of me. Going through the Pillars, I learned and realized that I am not going to get where I want in life or business if I don't take time out for me. I feel like I have made some improvements, thanks to Diane and this program. It is still a work in progress, but I can see the light at the end." ~Anneliese Dusseldorp

"I'm so glad I invested in the program. I have a book full of notes, more confidence, AND the big one, I pay more attention to self-talk, negative possibilities that haven't happened, how I 'show up,' how I react. This program has been a godsend! Whether you are a business owner or a woman, this is a great benefit. Thank you Diane!" ~Chantal Staaf

"Participating in the Dynamic You™ Program furthered my awareness of self sabotage and the role confidence plays in reaching my greatest potential. Stepping into the new role as a life & business coach I was allowing self-doubt to keep me small and hidden. I needed the extra push and training from Diane to give myself the confidence to be seen. After experiencing the Dynamic You™ Program I am advancing at a faster pace in growing my business by confidently connecting with other women."
~Pam Karlen

"Dynamic You™ was a well laid out, easy to follow program. Be committed, and prepared to do the work! Diane put into words many of the things I was trying to express. She pushed us (in the nicest way!) to grow and step into being our Dynamic selves. She reminded me to find those opportunities and experiences that make me SPARKLE. As women we need to continue to support and encourage each other and share our stories. She brings to life this quote from Glinda in The Wizard of Oz, You've always had the power my dear, you just had to learn it for yourself."
~Sandra Girard

"I have done many programs and Dynamic You™ has really been amazing. The program really challenges you to dig deeper to find your true purpose and Diane is an amazing coach. If you have not yet done so, I would register for the program." ~Fatima Sumar

"I have loved getting to know MYSELF better. A big heartfelt thanks to Diane for facilitating and creating the space for us to grow and step into being our Dynamic selves!" ~Tazeem Jamal PMDT, LE

"I LOVED being part of Dynamic You™ Program. I was eager to do the exercises and be part of the calls. I felt the Pillars were very practical, in the sense that I could APPLY each one to my current situation, personal or business. Being able to apply what I was learning right the way was crucial to keep me motivated and interested in learning more! I love structure, so to have tasks, homework and challenges REALLY worked for me. Learning other strong, intelligent women have similar struggles and even insecurities made me feel "normal" about my own. I have tears in my eyes as I write Dynamic You™ had a tremendous impact in my life and I will carry that with me for years to come. I even already made a "date with myself" to review the lessons. This program was a lifesaver and it will help me immensely as I push forward towards bigger goals in the next few years."
~Claudine Pender

Also by Diane Rolston

Key 2 Success (eBook)

Programs by Diane Rolston

Dynamic You™
Dynamic Year™
Dynamic Balance™
Dynamic Power™
Dynamic Catalyst™
She's Goaled™ Coaching Mastermind

Meet Diane Rolston online and receive free training at
www.DianeRolston.com

DYNAMIC YOU™

*The Secret Code To Being
Confident, Wealthy & Successful*

Unleash Your
Dynamic Woman™

DIANE ROLSTON

Copyright © 2017 Diane Rolston
All rights reserved.
ISBN: 1542468434
ISBN-13: 978-1542468435

DEDICATION

DEDICATED to all of you Dynamic Women™ out there! Women who lead the way, march to your own drum and stand in who you are rather than what you do. Women who consider themselves ordinary, but are truly extraordinary in their influence and legacy. To those who have gone before and challenged the norm to make things better and inspire our own impact.

Specifically to two Dynamic Women™ who have come before me, my Mother, Sheila, whose own story inspires me to take great leaps both on stage and in life and whose endless love gives me permission to do the same. And to my late Grandmother, Ethel, whose creativity inspires me and whose small business spirit runs through my veins.

CONTENTS

	Welcome Letter	1
1	Have Success with Dynamic You™	3
2	Pillar 1: Prioritized	17
3	Pillar 2: Be Real	30
4	Pillar 3: Connected	43
5	Pillar 4: Perspective	54
6	Pillar 5: Self-aware	63
7	Pillar 6: Be Magnetic	72
8	Pillar 7: Collaborate	85
9	Pillar 8: Be Confident	99
10	Pillar 9: Shine	120
11	Your Next Steps	135
	Dynamic You™ Program Participants	141
	Acknowledgments	146
	About the Author	147

Hello there, lovely!

I want to connect with you personally before you start this book. You are reading this for a specific reason. Do you know that reason? Of course you do! Consciously or unconsciously, something grabbed your attention. Have a little think about it right now. Did the title appeal to you? Did you hear me speak somewhere? Have you read something else I wrote? Are you looking to solve a problem? Are you looking to become more successful? Are you looking for new ways to reach your goals?

Whatever the reason, you have come to the right place. This book is for all women—and men too if they really want, but the examples are for women, the success stories are about women, and the book was written with women in mind.

I'm so excited to be sharing this book with you. How are you feeling about getting started? Are you excited? Are you nervous? Are you feeling both? That's completely normal, and I don't want you to worry. I am going to take care of you.

When reading this book, I want you to feel as though we are having a conversation, like when I'm working face to face with clients. I want you to know I am speaking to you, I am thinking of you, and that I am really excited and thrilled to be on this journey with you. It is my absolute honor that you trust me enough to take you through this process. You might be thinking, "Oh, I just wanted to read a book." Or maybe you're wondering, "What am I in for?" Let me tell you a little bit more about Dynamic You™.

So many women wish things could be different—that they could be different. I hear women wish for more confidence. They wish they could step out of the day-to-day and into what they truly want and feel more self-assured about it. They wish they could belong in every place and every situation. They wish obstacles felt easier and smaller. They wish their goals felt within reach. And they wish they had a reliable system by which to pursue these things so that nothing would get in their way. Do you feel any of this?

This is why I've created Dynamic You™. From years of coaching, I've pieced together my experience in leading over 200 workshops, facilitating countless Dynamic Women™ in Action events, and numerous speaking engagements. I have collected the knowledge I have acquired from all the women I've met through my events and through my international coaching clients. I have compiled every bit of invaluable information, putting it together into a six-week program—the very program through which I have trained hundreds of other women—and I have put that program into this book. So sometimes I will call Dynamic You™ a book and sometimes a program. Please know it's both.

You also get a lot of the comments from the ladies who went through the six-week Program. If you want to learn more about them and see their photos, turn to the back of the book. Basically this is a Program within a book, and its intention is to **UNLEASH the DYNAMIC WOMAN™ in YOU!**

I'm so excited to be sharing this with you, and like my clients, you will receive its multitude of benefits. Let's figure out exactly what you're going to be able to be, do, and have by reading this book.

By the end you'll be able to:

- Apply the Dynamic Women™ Code, so you're in control of your outcomes & boosting your opportunities
- Use the 9 Pillars to increase your overall satisfaction & success in all areas of life
- Ditch the labels, so you feel more confident
- Use guidelines to know how to be an equal in any situation
- Feel free by letting go of perfectionism and putting away your superwoman cape

The information in Dynamic You™ is the foundation on which I shifted my life, and since then, I've been living in brilliance and successfully realizing my goals. You can make the shift too! This book won't try to make you a different person—because you are not broken and I don't need to fix you. Instead, it will provide the tools you need in order to make a shift in your mindset, supporting your growth and ramping up what is possible so that you achieve better results. I feel blessed that I get to impact others and inspire them, and I'm so grateful for everyday I get to continue to live this DYNAMIC life.

Stay Dynamic!

Diane

Diane Rolston
Certified Premier Success Coach
International Speaker
CEO & Founder of Dynamic Women™ in Action

CHAPTER 1
HAVE SUCCESS WITH DYNAMIC YOU™

The Three Phases of Dynamic You™

1. Learning

In Phase One, you'll learn the Nine Pillars of being a Dynamic Woman™. I will teach you what they are, why they are important, and provide ways for you to apply them. I'll also share examples from my clients' lives and experiences. You'll hear how real women, just like you, have struggled with certain Pillars, overcame obstacles, and accomplished their goals after applying what they learned in this program.

Tip: Don't read through this book in one sitting. Structure your own reading of this book like the group programs I have instructed. We study and deeply understand one Pillar at a time. Ideally, with the book, you will read no more than one Pillar each week. This way, you will have enough time to internalize each Pillar and thoroughly benefit from its profitable lessons.

2. Awareness

As I have seen in my clients, simply learning the Nine Pillars creates a shift in thinking. You'll find different ways of looking at things, your experiences, and what role you played in creating them. Then, when you're ready to employ the suggestions in real life, you'll possess a deeper understanding of each Pillar, how it works best for you, and a greater awareness of your own part using it in the world.

3. Implementation

The best way to bring each of the Nine Pillars into your life is with a challenge. Challenges motivate us to make moves, gently pushing us out of our comfort zones. The intention is that by implementing an activity or challenge, we will be able to test and practice what we have learned.

You may feel a little anxious about being part of this journey and the dynamic change it will create in your life. Action will ease that anxiety. Anxiety comes from the unknown, from overthinking and under-doing. Once you get moving, and start acting instead of deliberating, you'll realize it wasn't as hard as you thought it would be. Trust me, I hear it from my clients all the time.

More often than not, our anxieties build obstacles up to be bigger than they really are. The cool thing is that our souls know we're capable of more, and that we want a deeper fulfillment and satisfaction from our lives. Your feelings are telling you something, listen to them. By using my clients' feelings as a compass, I can better support them along their journey.

Benefits of Dynamic You™

Focusing on being the Dynamic You™ produces seven clear benefits. By fully implementing Chapter One's Three Phases, you will have the opportunity to not only reap the Seven Benefits, but you will find hundreds if not thousands more. When you unleash the Dynamic Woman™ in you, the profits are endless. And the results for each Dynamic Woman™ are just as unique as your fingerprint—as your DNA.

This book is so powerful because it crosses generations, cultures, economic standing, religions, and all possible situations and backgrounds. It unites us.

1. Apply the Dynamic Woman™ Code

The first benefit of Dynamic You™ is that by the end of this book you'll be able to apply the Dynamic Woman's™ Code. This Code is the secret of successful, wealthy, and confident women all over the world. They take the Nine Pillars, and blending them together, they make a unique, personal code. The code is the foundation for all we do. It manifests in the way you feel, how you think, what you say, and how you act. It creates our results and our results become our reality.

2. Be In Control Of Your Outcomes

The second benefit is that you'll be in control of your outcomes. How is that? Aren't some things out of our control, you ask? Not exactly. From each Pillar, you will learn how to live life intently, and this intention guides your focus. By consciously designing relationships with others and the situations you find yourself in, you'll have a stronger say in how it all plays out. And when you take control, you'll also boost your opportunities.

3. Ditch the Labels

Labels, titles, and roles define us, and in some cases they are necessary. It's important to embrace one's role as a mother, a sister, a daughter, etc. But labels also keep us confined, judged, and working to live up to society's burdensome expectations. Instead, you're going to ditch the labels so that you can stand confidently in who you are, rather than in some job role or some other title you've been given. And after you ditch those unnecessary titles, others can't label you, and thus, won't constrict you anymore. You will feel free and able to truly be you.

4. Increase Your Satisfaction And Success

By covering these Nine Pillars, you're going to improve your results. And when you achieve better results, your confidence will improve along with those successes. And most importantly, so too will your overall satisfaction increase in all areas of life.

5. Know How To Be An Equal In Any Situation

Labels, titles and roles divide us and keep us apart. They only show us our differences, ultimately making us compare ourselves to each other. The Nine Pillars are equalizers. By learning them, you're going to use them to connect with others and learn how to be an equal in any situation. Then, when you begin implementing them, you'll see how they help you achieve better results.

6. No More Superwoman, No Need For Perfectionism

A superwoman is someone who works hard to manage multiple roles:

- An employee,
- a homemaker,
- a volunteer,
- a student,
- or other such time-intensive occupations.

Every day, superwomen juggle errands and domestic 'To Do' lists. They come home to laundry that needs sorting and washing, groceries that need buying and putting away, and homes that need cleaning. And I want to recognize that this is an issue for women whether they have children or not. It's also an issue for women whether they have a partner or spouse or not.

On your journey through the Nine Pillars, you'll be able to drop society's burden to be a superwoman, and ultimately, lessen the pressure to achieve perfectionism. That's going to help you to feel freer and a lot more confident.

7. Be Unapologetically You

I don't want to change who you are because you do not need to be someone else. And I don't want to add more demands or more stuff to your life. I just want you to be the most Dynamic You™ you can possibly be. That's a bit of a tongue twister. I want you to increase your satisfaction and build your own success. That way, you can't be labeled anymore. And if people try to label you, it won't diminish any of your power.

Thrive with Dynamic You™

With anything I do, I ask, "How I can do it more efficiently?" Efficiency is a value of mine because it saves me time and energy, and I'm sure you value your time and energy as well. You know the expression, "Time is money." But I actually believe that "Time is… everything!" We don't possess a limitless supply of time, and unfortunately, we can't recreate it either. It is a non-renewable resource. That's why I'm going to share with you how you can get the most out of your time by being the Dynamic You™. These ideas will enrich your experience, deepen what you learn, and ensure you obtain the results you are looking for.

Be Part of the Community!

I want you to know that sometimes, yes, you might not feel included in life. But with Dynamic You™, you're part of our Global Community! That means you get to connect with others who are reading the book just like you are now, those who have finished the book, and those who are already living the Dynamic Woman™ lifestyle.

You have the opportunity to share with the ladies, with my team and with me! Start off by joining the Dynamic You™ Global Community on Facebook. Just search for it and follow the directions to be added to the group. Then jump in and introduce yourself!

We'd love to know your:

- Name
- Location
- Your current titles Ex. Mom, CEO, Nurse (please no elevator pitches)
- What you love (from any area of your life)
- Why you're part of Dynamic You™ (see the next part for some ideas)
- Oh and don't forget to share what makes you a Dynamic Woman™! (Choose some adjectives: are you creative, playful, loving, decisive etc.)

Why Are You Here?

In Chapter One, I asked you why you're reading this book. Now I'd love for you to pull out a journal—and if you don't have a journal right now grab a piece of paper—and write down the answer to these questions. (Then schedule a time to go and buy a journal – hint hint!)

- What drew you to this book?
- What do you want to get out of this program?
- What is your intention?

The answers to these questions are crucial to getting the most out of Dynamic You™. By answering these questions, you can gain clarity regarding the results for which you're aiming. When you figure that out, I'd love for you to share it with me on our Facebook group as I mentioned before.

Here are some reasons why women like you joined the Dynamic You™ Program:

Pam Karlen shared, "I joined to be more dynamic when being seen (online and off) and to have the confidence to get my business out into the world. I had awesome results. Thank You Diane!"

Leagh Wright, "What drew me to the program was I really liked the idea of an in depth lengthy journey to grow and develop in a group of like minded women. I have outgrown some of my friends and looking forward to making some new ones that are like the new me. My intentions for the program are to focus on myself (which is new to me) and focus on my goals. Health and finances are at the top off my list in the short term."

Claire Madin, "My intention for the program is to grow, learn and challenge myself further to be more dynamic."

Cora Naylor, "To embrace my vulnerability at "putting myself out there" and not worry about what others may say. To hear but put aside the voices in my head telling me that I don't have what it takes and that I'm not qualified to do this."

Sandra Girard, "My intention for this program: to create some constancy and follow through with my new skin care business as well as my health. It seems I know what to do – it's the doing!

Maria Peebles, "I am doing this program because I want to focus on me, and how I can understand and improve myself, in turn hopefully helping my relationships and in all levels both personally and professionally."

Claudine Pender, "What drew me to the program (aside from the curriculum) was TRUST that what Diane had to share would change my life for the better. My intention was to say YES to the path the Universe was showing me and hope for some clarity in what to do next."

Elaine Tan Comeau, "Why am I doing this? I have never had a business coach or any type of coach. I would love to feel like I am not doing "this" all by myself. I would truly like for someone to grab me by the shoulders and shake me sometimes and make sure I have a reality check when I feel like I have too much going on or when I am not brave enough to jump. It would great to know that I am doing the right things and not just doing too many things and things that I should not be doing. I just feel like I get too distracted from achieving the end goal as fast as I should."

Sukeina Jethabhai, "What drew me to the program was an opportunity to have a coach. My biggest saboteur is self doubt--while I am very authentic and will speak my mind; I am constantly worrying about how I'm coming across and whether I'm good enough--I feel I have to prove myself. I also feel that I don't value myself and lack contentment."

Anneliese Dusseldorp, "My Intention for this program is to learn what it takes to be more confident to be Dynamic shining light to others and be a Dynamic Speaker."

Michelle Abraham, "My Intention for this program is the focus on me! Start making myself a priority so I can help others better. This starts with me. I do everything to do with kids, food, finances, medical appointments, getting up with the baby all night, housework etc. as well as trying to run a business, it doesn't leave anytime for me. I don't ask for help or delegate and I don't carve out time for workouts etc. so I am left feeling unsupported, exhausted and crappy for not exercising and resentful for not having someone magically step in and take on some things at home!"

Tazeem Jamal, "Why I am doing this? I want to really focus on prioritising ME & uplevel my results in my career, my income and to do that I must FOCUS on being the best version of me. What better way than to dig deep & grow with a community of supportive women!"

Fall Fast And Fall Often

We are all figuring out how we want to show up in this world and what we want to achieve. Know that this is a journey. You will fumble, make missteps, and maybe even decide that the path you originally intended on taking doesn't work for you anymore, and maybe you'll end up going another way. That's totally normal and completely expected. In fact, I actually encourage you to fall hard and to fall fast, because you are going to learn how to get up, wipe yourself off, and get going again.

Don't Play It Safe Here

Be sure to passionately invest in the program. If you plan on playing it safe, how are you going to unleash the Dynamic Woman™ in you? The whole word "dynamic" is about positive change, change that you make happen actively and intentionally. Try things on just as you would clothing in a fitting room. You can put it on, dislike it, and cast it aside. Apart from this book, you haven't purchased anything yet, but if you don't try it on first, you won't know if you want to buy it or not.

A friend of mine recently suggested I try wearing leopard print. I was sceptical at first because I don't usually wear animal print. But you know what? I tried it and I actually love it! I wore animal print earlier today and received several compliments on the wild shirt, leaving me feeling good about myself, brave, and ultimately more confident. But I wouldn't have felt that way if I had never tried it on in the first place. So hey, you never know. Open yourself up to doing and saying things outside your comfort zone. Open yourself up to a new and different way of being. I bet you will be pleasantly surprised with the results.

No Beating Yourself Up & No Judgments

I want to make it clear you do not need to become a different person. You are awesome! The point of this program is to foster that awesomeness in a positive way, turning up the good qualities and turning down the anxieties and things that aren't working as well for you. How does that sound? Are you open to that? Because if you want different results in your life, you need to be open to doing things differently. And in this coaching process, I'm going to teach you how.

As I said before, every woman is figuring out how and who she's going to be in this world. But when you are making those decisions, I want to make sure you're not hard on yourself. No beating yourself up. No judgments. When we do that, we are demanding perfection from ourselves, focusing on our inadequacies and questioning who we are. Instead, let's celebrate our great qualities. And if we possess a quality that isn't giving us the best results, we can choose to turn it down. For example, someone who's great at talking can dominate conversations, and someone who is great at listening will often remain silent. If both people just turned down that quality, there would be space to turn up the opposite quality and have a great conversation where both people share and are heard. Again, it's not about changing you. It's just about using your qualities in the right ways.

If at any point you feel a judgment coming on, please just write it down in your journal and share it with the online community. All you have to do is say, "Hey, I was thinking about the way that I am and now I'm judging this thing about myself." Let us know how you're feeling, take ownership of those feelings, and receive some affirmations from your Dynamic Woman™ Community. That's what the group is for. Let the other women hear you and cheer you on. There could even be an opportunity for me to join in on the conversation and give you a little bit more coaching. Sound good?

Be Authentic, Be Real & Be You

As you go through the Pillars, you may experience a lack of confidence, you may feel awkward or uncomfortable, but just keep going. The trouble is we feel it's hard to be authentic and real because we're always trying to be someone else or we're trying to do or act or say things in a way that is uniform to everyone around us. Don't! Apply the Pillars in your way, with your style to your own life.

I'll be real with you about something I struggled with for a long time. I'm a crier. I cry easily at funerals. I cry when someone else is upset. I cry when someone has hurt me or when I'm disappointed. I can even dry at a 30 second commercial. I used to feel ashamed of it. Now I see it as a gift because I can cry when no one else will, giving permission for others to cry if they need. And when I cry for someone else at a time when they can't muster the tears (ex. the loss of a loved one), it will actually give them relief. Instead of considering crying a weakness, I now recognize that it's one of my superpowers.

Another quality I once considered to be weakness is that I speak my truth. I tell my clients what they need to hear, I tell friends what no one else will tell them. If you have broccoli in your teeth, I will let you know. I'm that person. Why? I strongly believe in positive outcomes. I speak up when values are being dishonored, whether those values belong to others or me.

- When someone takes another's spot, doesn't let someone else add to the conversation, or takes all of the credit—I speak up because it isn't fair.

- When a room is too cold at a conference for the attendees, or people can't see something—I tell the organizer because I care for the wellbeing of others.

- When someone speaks poorly about another person, situation, or even of themselves—I let them know it's not helping, asking them to reframe her criticisms because constructive feedback is always better than judgment.

- When a client is giving an excuse or not doing what they truly desire—I speak the hard truth in order to get them back on track.

It comes down to polar opposites. I have a mix of vulnerability and strength, heart and courage. You have unique gifts as well. You have a unique way of being and a unique purpose in the world. It's how you and I show up that makes the difference.

If we don't use our gifts honestly and energetically, people are going to know something is off. I encourage you to step into the best of who you truly are. Be authentic. Be real. Be yourself. Don't say something because you think I or anyone else wants to hear it. Don't. Don't do it in the program and don't do it in your life.

Write this down in your journal:

"Be authentically myself and be authentically real."

Great. Okay, let's keep going.

Dealing with the Saboteur

At times the saboteur is going to come out. Some people call it negative self-talk or the devil on your shoulder. It's that little voice in your head that holds you back, tells you negative things and tries to keep you "safe". We all have listened to this mental negativity before. Maybe you'll recognize some of these voices. It says things like:

"They're going to laugh at you."

"You'll fail."

"You don't fit in anyway."

"You don't have enough experience, time, money, connections etc."

Why Does The Saboteur Come Out?

Our saboteurs exist to keep us "safe" from things that pose an immediate threat to our safety. In womankind's early history, the saboteur was good for things like preventing us from getting mauled by a tiger, or helping us avoid starvation and extreme cold. In modern times, the saboteur keeps us safe from things like a masked gunman or a truck coming at us on the sidewalk. Unfortunately, the saboteur tries to keep us safe from all things that makes us feel even slightly uncomfortable all the way to stressed, like standing on stage, calling a potential client, or having a difficult conversation with a loved one. The saboteur's job is to keep us safe, and its negative voice starts talking when our bodies' stress responses are activated. The problem is that the saboteur can't tell the difference between life-threatening dangers like a tiger and merely anxiety-inducing situations like speaking up during a meeting.

I've had clients whose saboteur comes out even during positive experiences, like giving an acceptance speech for a great award or getting a promotion. Saboteurs come out for small things too, like writing a blog or sending an email. Anything that takes us out of our easy comfort zone brings out the saboteur. Day in and day out, it will try to keep you in a safe little bubble by saying negative things to prevent you from growing out and beyond that confined space.

How Do You Beat The Saboteur?

Write down what the saboteur is saying, because when you do, you'll see that it's only information. If they say that you don't look good or people are not going to listen to you, whatever it is, write it down and then post it. Where? On the Facebook Community. Why? You'll find others have the same saboteurs saying similar things. You'll feel understood and completely normal in your experience. Then you can share how you've been combating your saboteurs and learn tips from others.

The saboteur is separate from you. You are not telling yourself these judgmental things. It's the saboteur trying to keep you safe, but you know better. It's your job to tell the saboteur to be silent and let you live your life the way you see fit. And don't worry, if a tiger comes your way, the saboteur will still be there and will know what to do. I want you to grab any truth in what they are saying. Maybe you're worried you don't have enough experience. If that is in fact true, then great! Go and gain some more experience. This program will only help you to expand in that area.

By stepping into your Dynamic You™, you're going to be able to let go of the saboteur's hold. You will be able to really hear and understand what your inner cues are telling you. And instead of feeling lost or wanting more, you are going to feel satisfaction in yourself because you are going to live who you are to the fullest.

Being a Dynamic Woman™

I trust you're all ready to go with your journal, and that you understand the ways in which to get the most out of Dynamic You™. Now's the time to talk about being a Dynamic Woman™, because in Dynamic You™, we are unleashing the dynamic woman in you.

Who Is A Dynamic Woman™?

Well, you are, of course! We all are! We are all Dynamic Women™ and it's important we recognize that for ourselves. When I asked women in the last program they answered, "I'm a dynamic woman because I'm funny, I'm putting myself out there, I'm always working on something new, I'm never standing still, I have boundless energy, I love change."

Now that you have a few examples of what you might say, let me define it a bit more—a dynamic woman. It's funny, when I started Dynamic Women™ in Action (DWA™), I tried to come up with a word that could encompass all kinds of women, the shy ones and the outgoing ones, the professionals and the business women, the moms and the non-moms. I wanted to think about everybody, every type, any age, any demographic. Something that was all-inclusive so that no woman would feel like, "Oh, that's not me and so I can't be part of that."

The excitement of the word "dynamic" launched out of creating DWA™. The word "dynamic" is powerful, and it's active. It means a variety of things, encompassing many different qualities within it, and that's why I really love the word.

Being a dynamic woman embodies all talents and all skills. Anytime I launched a new location (I launched eight locations in British Columbia), I found that during the activity where I asked the women, "What makes a woman dynamic?" — words like sassy, vivacious, free, carefree, loving, organized and so many other exciting words came out of them. You name it, qualities, skills, talents, beliefs, someone named it. Each group had its own list, its own way of doing it, from contrasting words to ranges of scale. They had everything you could possibly imagine. The women also delved into how people did things, not only descriptions of who they were. You get to be everything, not boxed in. Check out the photos in the Facebook Group to see posters of the words the women shared.

A Dynamic Woman™ focuses on who she is, not titles nor what she does. She shows up as a dynamic woman; i.e., authentically herself. Maybe you've been to an event where somebody comes in the room and you go, "Oh, I need to know her." Or someone is talking in a group and you think, "She seems to be the person to know." Or it could even have been a quiet person sitting at a table, but still you think, "Hey, there's something mysterious about her. I need to meet her." Any of those times when you've felt that kind of magnetic pull towards someone, that's a Dynamic Woman™. Just like that, I want everyone to be able to be dynamic in every situation.

The last part about being a Dynamic Woman™ is the essence they make you feel when you're around them. Not only how you see them from afar, but how you feel when they are near. That sensation you feel when in a flowing conversation with them, when you want to know more about them because they are so interesting and there's a positive vibe between you two.

This code I mentioned is the equalizer. Dynamic Women™ are all these qualities, but they also embrace change. There's change in all areas of life. We're changing every single day. You might not notice, but change is happening everywhere—all around you. Don't be afraid of change. Think of it more as growing or stepping fully into who you are. You can try to control these things, or you can embrace change. And I'll tell you, embracing change is so much easier than trying to keep things the same. Because you can't keep things the same.

To recap, here are the five things that make a woman dynamic:

1. They encompass many talents and skills.
2. They focus on who they are rather than what they do.
3. When they show up, you know they're dynamic.
4. The way you feel around this woman is super awesome.
5. They embrace change.

Who Made The Rules?

The sad thing is, we think there are unspoken rules we must follow in order to be accepted. Who made these rules anyway? Rules where you must be a certain way, dress and look a certain way, talk a certain way. As a mom you're this way, as a wife, you're that way, and as a business owner, you're another way. Man! There are so many guidelines and nonsense rules to follow. No pressure or anything, right?! Well, I'm going to create a simpler path. The problem with those rules is they're confining. If you dance to the beat of a different drum, then it's really hard to follow any one path. The joy is that we get to recreate them. You like design? You like being creative? Perfect. It's your chance to redesign things.

Again, we're going to ditch society's titles, labels, and roles, including ones from our jobs, our families, our upbringing, and any other titles from the past that we've had. Even the positive labels that you might have embraced because you performed really well under them and maybe were even rewarded for them. Let them all go.

For a while I shared with others that I was the finalist for the 2014 Leading Moms Award, which was a great honor, but it boxed me into being a mom who leads. What if I wanted to be a business owner who collaborated? When 2016 came along, I thought, well that award was from 2014. That's two years ago! So I can't really claim that title anymore. I am not defined by my titles and neither are you! I am so much more now, and while it was such a great honor to be a finalist, it's just not something that is defining me right now.

It's funny, when I go travelling, and when I go away, I get to show up as whoever I want to be. Maybe you have experienced this as well. If you wanted to pretend like you're more outgoing, then you could. If you wanted to be more carefree, then you can. I know that when I was younger and I traveled (before having kids), my motto was saying "yes!" to any wonderful opportunity. By wonderful opportunity, I mean the canyon swing, bungee jumping, horseback riding, glacier hiking, skydiving, these kinds of adventurous activities. I was focused on growing, on stepping out of my boundaries while embracing challenge and risk taking.

If you could redesign or choose how you want to show up in a new place where no one knows who you are, who would you be? That's your next, deeper thought question. Who would you be? If you could just show up somewhere and be whomever you wanted, what would she look like? What would she say? How would she carry herself? Again, go ahead and share that on the Facebook Community.

Please know it's the educator in me who encourages you to post because I know the benefits of sharing. And the coach in me can then support you better. Of course, feel free to post other things too, but I know reading a book can often be a passive activity, so let's make it more active.

Now some titles we can't change easily. For example, job titles, citizenship, being a wife. Rather than only dealing with being put in a box, what you can change or what you can say is, who am I now? And who do I want to be? That's why we're going to look at who you could be if you were going somewhere new. Basically, I want you to be unapologetically you, the Dynamic You™. And the code I'm going to teach you is an equalizer. Does that sound good?

CHAPTER 2
PILLAR 1: PRIORITIZED

Now is the time for us to talk about the very first Pillar of stepping into your most dynamic self. Are you ready for it? Dynamic Women™ Prioritize themselves.

What Does It Mean To Be Prioritized?

Life has many demands, and all of them, including our loved ones, are competing for our attention. All of them deserve our full attention when we are with them, but prioritizing yourself is crucial. It's actually a form of self-love. When you love yourself enough to decide that you too will receive an equal amount of time, energy, and resources—know that you deserve it.

A lot of people love themselves, but that doesn't mean they prioritize themselves. I asked the ladies in my first Dynamic You™ Program if they prioritized themselves, and 80% of the women I talked with said that they were at the bottom of their priority list. About 10% said they weren't even on their own list at all. What's that about?

The issue I found is that women feel it's selfish to prioritize themselves, that they fulfill a role or a job title, meaning they have to sacrifice themselves to do a good job. But that's simply not true. They don't need to. There is a balance within all of it. Women are acknowledged for being selfless, giving, loving, doing for others, nurturing. It's part of the role we play as women.

What's getting in the way? Shortage of sleep? The agendas of others? Lack of self-care? Monitor your routine so that you can see what adjustments need to be made.

A client of mine was sick and didn't feel she had the time to prioritize herself or her health. Instead, she felt she needed to focus on getting things done for other people because some of her time was lost due to her sickness. When she started to feel better, she felt the need to catch up with her work, housework and errands rather than exercise. This is the time she **needed** to prioritize herself. Basically, you are never too busy for five minutes. Five minutes is manageable. If you don't make the time for yourself, you will fill it with other things regardless.

Be Self-Full

I must clarify the difference between self-sacrifice and choosing yourself. There's a very big difference. A lot of people sacrifice themselves for others, but actually choosing yourself is the way to go. I'm not in any way saying to be selfish, but instead to be "self-full". Full of love and care for ourselves, which means prioritizing ourselves.

The truth is we can't give unless we have something within ourselves from which to give. You can't withdraw from a bank account if you have never deposited. Unless you are self-full, you won't have a full cup, and without a full cup you'll have nothing to pour out for others. You've probably heard many people say this before in personal development, but I'll say it again, in case of an emergency on an airplane, you put your oxygen mask on first, and then you help others with theirs. We feel it's okay to do that in an emergency situation, so why not in day-to-day life?

In life, very rarely do we give ourselves the time, attention, and care that we need. I know because I am guilty of it too. I have to put myself in check. You know that before you can be there for anyone else, you have to be there for yourself. I've seen it many times over. And if you're not choosing yourself, other people will choose themselves over you. I'll say that again. Other people will choose themselves over you. Some people say, "Oh, he walks all over me," or, "They just expect this of me," or, "No one ever offers." Well, if you have said any of these then you've trained them to be that way. You've trained them to think not think of you as a priority because maybe you don't believe you need to be a priority.

If you're not choosing yourself, they're not choosing you either. So if you're not choosing you, and they're not choosing you, no one is choosing you. That is a sad realization.

How Do You Go About Prioritizing Yourself?

First, you have to be clear about what you NEED and what you WANT in all areas of life. "Areas of life?" you ask? See the Wheel of Life below: a professional coaching tool I use with my clients to gage their satisfaction in life. Not their success, but how satisfied they are in all areas, not only life and business.

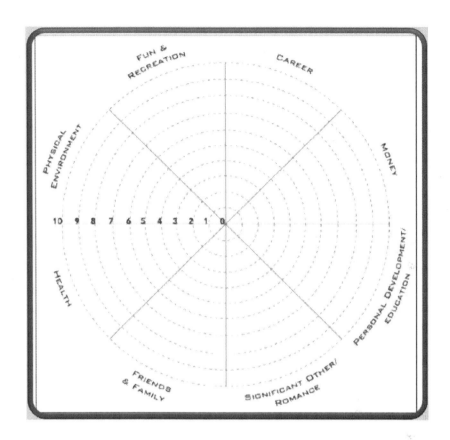

What Are Needs And Wants?

The needs come from the basics of what is necessary for you to live and to live healthfully. The wants should come from a higher place, and include more things you think are ideal. The wants might feel like a stretch, and you know what, that's perfect! For example, in health, you could say, "What I need is at least six hours of sleep, but what I want is eight hours, and ideally I want those hours to be from 10pm-6am." In your career you could say, "I need a consistent and stable job that pays me $70,000. However, I want a job that pays me closer to six figures and I also want to work from home. Ideally, I would also be travelling to other countries and take five weeks off a year."

That's what I want you to start thinking about. What's the ideal? What's that stretch? What's that wish or dream place?

So in the next table, write down what you need and what you want in all areas. That's not too difficult, is it? For some people, it might feel hard because they've never done it before or haven't in a long time. Now is your chance. Even if you did it last week, do it again. You may be surprised by new answers, and even if the same answers come out, it will be a good exercise to confirm what you know you want.

Here is how you're going to apply this.

1. Think about every area of life in the table.
2. Go through all the areas and write down (in the table) what you need in each area.
3. Then write down what you want in each area. Ask yourself – What is ideal?

Area of Your Life	Need	Want (What is Ideal?)
Career	1. 2. 3.	1. 2. 3.
Money	1. 2. 3.	1. 2. 3.
Personal Development/ Education	1. 2. 3.	1. 2. 3.
Spiritual Life	1. 2. 3.	1. 2. 3.

Significant Other/ Romance	1. 2. 3.	1. 2. 3.
Friends	1. 2. 3.	1. 2. 3.
Family	1. 2. 3.	1. 2. 3.
Health	1. 2. 3.	1. 2. 3.
Physical Environment	1. 2. 3.	1. 2. 3.
Fun and Recreation	1. 2. 3.	1. 2. 3.

This is the first part, where we build the foundation with which the Pillars will help you achieve your goals. Once you know what you need and want, you can use the Pillars to make it happen. And you'll have definitive reasons to prioritize yourself in every area of life.

Go back through all the things you need and want, and over the course of the next few days, see how many of those things you can implement and write down how it goes. This is the second part of the process—implementing your needs and wants into your life.

Here Is Your Challenge

Now, here's the part where we implement a challenge. ME-TIME. Prioritizing yourself through me-time—time where you get to do what you want to do. This isn't, "Oh, I spent some time cleaning," or, "I spent some time studying for this program I'm doing." Those don't count. Me-time is something that you're doing that's just for your own joy, just for your happiness. My me-time is often a long bath. Maybe it's coloring. It's reading a book. It's going for a hike, not stuff that's already a task in my normal life. It's a little bit beyond normal. I promise you that you can make the time to do it everyday. Honestly, ten minutes, five minutes, or it could just be taking something you already do and making it a little nicer for yourself. Instead of a quick coffee as you're working or running through your day, why don't you just take five minutes and sit on your patio, enjoying that cup of tea or coffee or water or whatever you're having in blissful me-time.

Carve out me-time every day, and as I said, it can be ten minutes, five minutes or just changing a thing you would normally do for yourself and make it a little bit sweeter. Do you enjoy your facial routine? Spend a little extra time intently exfoliating and massaging in that moisturizer. Do you enjoy cooking? Skip the canned tomatoes and opt for chopping, seasoning, and blistering the fresh ones.

Who Are You Doing Things For?

When you look at every area and every situation with others and examine what they are asking, you will discover when and where you are giving more than necessary. Where are you expected to pick up everyone else's slack? Ask yourself, are you doing it because you offered or because you're expected to do it? Are you giving too much? Are you giving to the point where there's nothing left over for yourself?

Are you going out of your way to make things easier for someone else? Because then you are probably making it harder for yourself.

Do not worry if you've created the situation, because you can redesign it. If you've trained people in your life to be that way, then you can retrain them not to be. But it starts with you being clear about your needs and ideal wants. I promise you, it won't harm the relationship. Instead, you will be allowing them to step up. You're inviting them to lean in and do more. Their reaction is their choice, and you are not responsible for it.

Let's Do A Recap

The first part of this process is figuring out what your needs and wants are regarding the different areas of your life. Then, you're going to take those needs and wants and see how you can apply them this week. And the challenge is to carve out some me-time every day. And finally, please share in the Dynamic You™ Global Community how it went.

Intentionally notice and write down in your journal. Capture how you felt when asking for what you needed, and how it felt asking for what you wanted. Ask yourself, how did I feel about implementing what I need and what I want? Did I take me-time? What was my story, my inner dialogue? What did my inner saboteur's voice say? What did it say during me-time? Did it sound like any of the following: "I just don't have time for this." "I've got a lot to do." "There's a lot that needs to get done." "My kids need me." "I have a deadline." Were these things in any of your inner dialogue? You need to write it down so you can really bring the Pillar in strong.

Share with the Community something that happened. Share an example of where you successfully employed a Pillar. Share how it felt while learning to ask for what you need or what you want. How did it feel to take that me-time every day? Participating in our Facebook group, sharing stories, posting your experiences and your successes, and applying this Pillar of making yourself a priority will help you get so much more out of this program. Additionally, your story could be featured in my future books or new editions of this one. And of course, I will always ask for your permission before I share anything publically. Please, I encourage you to participate. I want to share your stories with other women out there, because just as you will learn from them, they will learn from you too.

Promise? Promise you'll do that?

Not for me, but for you. I would hate for you to invest in reading this book and not get everything you can from it. I want that for you. I know the material in this book will create positive changes for you. This book is going to help you step into that Dynamic You™. I know because I work one-on-one with women all the time and I see it happening in them.

Over the next weeks, that's what we're going to do. But it will only work if you're committed and intently following along. I applaud you again for taking this step. I really appreciate the fact that you trust me to serve you, and I'm so excited to see the growth that you will be celebrating at the end. I am so grateful to be a part of every step of this process, your journey.

As I mentioned earlier, this book isn't meant to merely be read from cover to cover. Now is a great time to put the book down and start the activities. Live in Pillar One for a while, and then come back to the book. That is how I designed the program. There is a week between each of the Pillars.

Pillar One Check-in

How did you do with making yourself a priority? If you were to score yourself on a scale of one to ten, what would you give yourself?

Remember earlier when I asked the ladies in my first Dynamic You™ Program how they prioritized themselves, and 80% of the women said they felt as though they were at the bottom of their own priority list? And about 10% aren't even on their own list?

TIME is the biggest reason why women struggle with Pillar One. They feel there is too much to do. That other things take priority, that other people take priority. Things like cleaning the house, working, caring for their families, etc.

A client of mine, shared that, "Saying no and putting [yourself] first is really empowering when you haven't ever done it before." She has a new perspective and a new toolset for making me-time a top priority.

Once you get the hang of making me-time for yourself every day, it's time to start taking some me-days, or what I like to call, "days of no responsibility." On me-days, you decide what to do with the entire day. Read, write a letter to grandma, take a nap, cook, call a friend, shop, paint, or even clean out your junk drawer if that's what you really want to do.

The Pillar Challenge was to take some me-time. How was that? How did it feel? What was your inner dialogue? What did the saboteur say?

Did you feel like you ran out of time to fit it in? Here is what I have found works really well. Prioritize yourself early in the morning so that other people's agendas don't become prioritized over your own. The day can get away from you. The worst thing is to put yourself at the end of your priority list again and again, because fires you need to extinguish come your way throughout the day, and you might be tempted to give up your me-time to fit it all in.

Chantal Staaf, "Woke up earlier this morning so I could go for a walk. As I am not much of a reader I sat still and enjoyed half hour of TV without doing laundry, answering texts nothing - me time. Tried the 6 min version of the Miracle Morning as well. Today is going to be a great day!!!"

Maria Westerhold Peebles, "Last night I went to restorative/deep stretch yoga. And had a very sound sleep! As I got home late, I planned to not get up early this morning. And yesterday I did start preparing for mornings. I downloaded a mediation app for my phone. Downloaded the 2 free chapters of Miracle Morning, and ordered the book from Amazon."

Pam Karlen, "To begin with my night plan to have a successful morning plan:
#1 unplug all electronics at 9:00 - bed at 10:00
#2 no caffeine late in day
#3 B12 (I have some will start taking it)
#4 read The Miracle Morning (I had it in my kindle already)
#5 stop reading at 9:00 so I can unplug."

Another client shared how she often will only prioritize herself when she hits the bottom and even then she gets fazed with how it will impact others. Worrying about everyone else is a paralyzer.

If you hit rock bottom, remember you have the tools, but are you brave enough to take the leap?

You could be further ahead if you don't procrastinate. Ask yourself what is that costing you? Self-awareness of what you really want and desire helps you to make decisions earlier and then get further on your path. At this point don't hold any guilt or judgment for not making a previous decision or action. You made that decision at that moment with the resources you had and as the person you were.

The sad thing is if you judge and prejudge yourself, when do you get to be awesome? You don't! You are sitting in "I did all of these things terribly so I don't trust myself in the future." How would it be if you just focused on the present?

The key is to use the Pillars, they are your tools so stand in their power. Then you can trust in yourself and when you trust in yourself your confidence grows which will then give you better results. But you have to be willing to put in the work. You are worth it! Create the space, mark it in your calendar, set your intention and stick to it.

Sukeina Jethabhai, "Prioritizing Me... I have been fortunate that I do have a supportive family and it has not been too difficult in prioritizing myself. I recently tipped the scale in a negative way and have made exercising a priority recently. Last week I was able to go to the gym about 4/7 days, which is awesome, and I am also working on my diet. The other change I have made is trying to not commit too much outside of my work and home life. I'm trying to focus on core priorities --me and getting my site set up (although the site set up is slow) and also getting some parts of our home life running smoothly.

"Waking up in the morning has not been easy and I have not been successful with this, but I'm choosing to forgive myself in this area and work on improving this."

The Miracle Morning™

I like to follow The Miracle Morning™. It comes from a book by the same name written by Hal Elrod. You can use this as a tool for self-care. Its structure sets you up for success, with adjustable times and the community to support you. By using The Miracle Morning™ routine, in as little as six minutes you can have powerful results. It's true!

With two kids under five-years-old, I needed something to help me focus on me. The Miracle Morning™ helps me feel more grounded, patient, healthy, and it gives me more time to make more things happen in all areas of my life.

The basic idea is that you get up early and start your day with the Life Savers.

The Lifesavers:

S – Silence

A – Affirmations

V – Visualization

E – Exercise

R – Reading

S – Scribe

I have been doing it for a while now and I love it. It has even stopped me from going to bed late (most nights) and I make better decisions about late night snacking so I can sleep well. Cool opportunities are coming my way, and it's had a positive impact on some of my closest relationships. I've been telling all of my clients about it, and I hope you also give it a try. You can download the first two chapters of The Miracle Morning™ free from their website.

To be transparent, there are times when 'night-Diane' screws over 'morning-Diane'. So 'morning-Diane' needs to set a schedule for 'night-Diane to follow'. You too can make this happen.

There might also be stages in your life where you feel the need to do it all and take everything on. But then you are taking on another large role and title. A client of mine was happily running her business and caring for her family, and then it was decided that for financial reasons she needed to go back to work fulltime. She was busier than ever, and so we had to devise a plan for her to go into maintenance mode in some areas of her life. Ultimately she remained the top priority, along with her health.

In your life, when have there been times where instead of ramping it up, it would have been better to go into maintenance mode?

We need time and space away from others in order to properly do this for ourselves. Often women are caring for others rather than having true free time. Kids are around, we are still seeing that all of the household chores are finished, and that our partners have their needs met too.

You need time away from your roles and responsibilities in order to gain insight and depth into your self-care. You need to be a priority. You need to know that you are worthy of being a priority, so that when you take on bigger challenges, you have the confidence to step into them.

If you still feel like you don't have enough time to do everything else in your schedule, track your time and tasks. I recommend Toggl as an online time-tracking tool. This will help you to see how you are spending your time. Then you can make choices regarding where your time is spent, and decide if you are using your time in the best way possible.

Don't get into the habit of saying you don't have enough time. It's a feeling of scarcity and helplessness, and from this place comes overwhelming feelings of stress and anxiety. Say to yourself, "I have enough time." Write it down. "I have enough time."

Bottom line, ask yourself—is this the most important thing I could be doing right now? Then make a decision to proceed with or stop that task. This is only going to work if you want it to, if you take action to make it happen.

Another client of mine said she only wanted twenty minutes to herself, but the trouble was she was distracted. When I asked her what she was distracted by, she replied, "My phone". People called her, texted her, and her Facebook and email notifications were going off like crazy. She felt that everyone treated her as though she were a "right now" kind of person.

That's how she trained them to treat her.

But she's not an ER doctor or on-call in any way, so there was no need for her to be available 24/7. In order to retrain the people around her—how to treat her and to create boundaries—we decided that she would just simply let them know she won't be available all the time. The key to getting some silence and time away from the phone is to put it on airplane mode.

Do you work in an office or from home? Either way, if others frequently interrupt you, let them know your office hours. Or choose another cue like closing the door, wearing headphones, or even put up a "busy" sign.

Additionally, new moms and busy moms often come last, and so it's imperative that they design time for themselves—time where they can be kid free and even responsibility free. This will require tremendous support from people around them, and they must not be shy to ask for it.

Claudine's update, "I now realize I want to make videos, go for walks and set up morning and night routines! I DID drink my tea and read my book today! I put my cell on airplane mode! All was well!"

Acknowledgment Time

I do want to acknowledge you for reading this, for the great work you've done answering the questions and taking on the Pillar Challenge. If you logged into the Facebook page and shared some of the things I asked you to share, even better! If you commented on other people's posts, fantastic. The part of this book, which requires you to connect with other Dynamic Women™, is super important. If you did all these things, I want to acknowledge you for participating, for taking this seriously, and for getting the most out of this book, just like those in the program do.

The more you engage, the more I can personally give you. The more you share, the more specific feedback and coaching you will receive from me. The more you share and connect with other women, the deeper the community you are building and the more connected you're going to feel. These will all give you the feeling that other people are similar to you and you're going to get more inspiration from them.

If that's the kind of experience you want to create, if you want to fully step into your Dynamic You™, participate. Show up. Be part of it. If you're already feeling like you're doing everything, that's awesome. But I invite you to step it up even further. What would that look like? What's that extra little step? Think about that.

In Pillar One, we talked about how Dynamic Women™ prioritize themselves. What's important about that? Many things.

1. First of all, when you prioritize yourself, other people catch on and start prioritizing you as well.

2. When you prioritize yourself by giving yourself me-time, which was our challenge, you build up your self-worth and the feeling that you deserve it.

3. It's also going to start to change how and when you say "yes" or "no" to things.

Continue to share how the first challenge is going. You don't just stop because we're moving on to Pillar Two. You're going to continue it for the duration of this book and beyond.

Every Pillar is going to build on the last one. Make sure you continue to apply each Pillar, keep using each Pillar, and let me and the Dynamic Community know how it's going. At this point, you've had some time in Pillar One; i.e., being prioritized. I encourage you to go on to the Facebook thread that asks you to share your success stories about Pillar One. If you can't find it, just do a quick search on the page for "Pillar One". There are very specific questions I have outlined, and I would love, love to hear how it went. Where you started, how the process was for you, what you learned, what you thought, how you felt, what obstacles you faced, and then in the end, where you're at with some success stories and your experience.

As you go through the book, feel free to go back and edit that Facebook post. Add more. Add more depth, and know that for my books and programs, this is where I pull success stories. No, I'm not just going to grab them without your permission. I'm going to look at them all and I'm going to choose some for each of the Pillars that I feel give readers hope, learning or inspiration. I might even end up setting a new kind of challenge for them base don your feedback. I'm going to do that for all the Pillars, all nine of them. So, comment on all of them! I would love to be able to showcase you and what you have been through, learned, your successes, the obstacles, whatever it is. Sound good?

CHAPTER 3
PILLAR 2: BE REAL

It's time for Pillar Two. Yeah! What's Pillar Two? Dynamic Women™ are real. So often I've heard and seen women acting like other people instead of being real regarding what they want, what they need or who they are. Each one of us was made the way we are for a reason. We possess unique talents and gifts to share with the world, and if we change our purpose, then we change the legacy we were meant to leave.

Think for a moment, why do you think people do this? Look to your family, your group of friends, your colleagues. I want you to think right now, why do you act this way? I'm going to say everybody at some point has, is, or will not act like the real them. Do you have your own special causes? I'm going to give you five reasons women, in particular, will do this.

5 Reasons Why Women Aren't Real

1. The first one is **to fit in**. Maybe they're in a new group of people, a new networking group, or a very specific group. To be part of that group, they feel they need to act like everyone else to fit in.

2. Second reason is **to connect**. By saying certain things, talking about certain things, acting a certain way, they're going to feel like they're connecting with people. There is some fault in that and I'll explain after.

3. Next is **to protect themselves**. They feel that if they share a bit too much it will affect their credibility or their business, or in some way impact their lives. Women aren't real because they try to protect themselves and what they have.

4. Next is they're **scared what others will think**. If they state their opinion or say something about their habits, they fear other people are going to think, "Oh my gosh. I'm judging her. Totally." And maybe push them out of the group or the circle.

5. The last reason is that women believe that merely **following along is easier** than creating their own paths.

Are any of these true for you? I've had experiences where I definitely felt like I needed to be somebody else. And so, I want to ask you, right now, when have you not been the real you? When have you faked it? Was it a particular business meeting? Was it with specific people? Was it when you attended something? When have you not been the real you? That's your next share on the Dynamic You™ Community. When have you not been the real you?

In order to switch from not being the real you to showing up authentically, I'm going to go into some reasons why you are actually hurting yourself when you do not act real.

5 Reasons Why Not Being Real Is Hurting You

1. It Stops You From Getting Out There

The first reason is when you're not real, it actually prevents you from getting out there. Because maybe in one situation you're this one way, and then you go over to another place and you act differently to fit in. Well, if some of those same people are in both locations, they will catch you out and not trust you. And for you personally, you feel confused as to how you show up in one place and how you show up in another. How do you know which person to be in which place? That confusion can lead to you not showing up at all, either at one of them or both, so it stops you from getting out there. Maybe you also think, "Oh my gosh, I'm going to have to take on another persona." Not cool. That's one reason it's not good to not be real.

2. It's Tiring

You know when you say one white lie and then you need another one to cover that story, and then cover that story, and then you start to forget what you said in the first place? Well, it's the same kind of thing. If you're showing up and thinking, "Oh, I have to be this way and I have to think about it and oh my gosh. What did I say last time and how do I need to be?" It is tiring. Pretending to be someone other than you is exhausting. If you haven't felt that, I'll let you know that when I started out coaching, and when I was younger, I've been in situations where I've felt like I needed to act a certain way. It even happens to me every once in a while now, and I need to catch myself, because otherwise, I'm not in sync and it doesn't feel good.

3. Pressure

This one stems from the last one. You feel pressure. You feel pressure to perform, to be at a certain place in our career, to reach a specific level of success, to have achieved this, earned that, parent the perfect kids, keep the best house, body, appearance, and partner. Compare-itis (the disease of comparing yourself to others) sets in, and it leads us into the next reason.

4. Stress

Pressure brings stress. Pressure brings dis-ease or disease. Right? It brings on illnesses. It can raise your cortisol levels. It can give you all the negative illnesses through mental, emotional, and physical stress like adrenal fatigue, anxiety, migraines, heart disease and tons of other symptoms. Not good.

5. You're Not In Line

At the core, you're not going to feel in line with who you are. You're not going to feel sincere, authentic, or like yourself. Instead, you'll feel artificial, and the truth is you can only sustain it for a very short amount of time. It's short-lived. But if you're the real you, you can be this way forever. Right? For as long as you are around.

My client, *Angela Foran* says, "It's hard to connect with others when I'm not being real because I'm always thinking, oh how should I say this or what should I say, so I'm always in my head rather than being present in what is happening at the moment. But, when I'm being real things flow better. I've had feedback in my job that I need to be different. I needed to be more entertaining, but that doesn't feel like the real me." I can see how putting on a flashy personality would be hard for *Angela*. She's a chill, laid-back woman who is so knowledgeable in what she does.

Sometimes for our role in a job, we do need to make a few changes to how we show up so we can perform to the best of our ability and provide for that which the job asks. For example, if you are a shy person, but in your job you need to go out and meet people, interview people, or if you're playing music on a stage, then you might feel uncomfortable. In *Angela's* case, she was able to change that part of her job rather than changing who she was.

So, here's a hard question, maybe. Maybe it is. Maybe it isn't. But it's a good coaching question for you.

Where are you putting on a fake front? Where are you not real?

Share your answer on the Dynamic You™ Global Community Page. Hey, there's no judgment here. Not being real is used as a tool, a technique for yourself, and maybe you just don't know another tool or technique that you can use instead. That's what I'm going to be giving you.

You have two questions so far. Let me keep going. Now, what I really want you to be thinking about is the reason you are not being real: Is because you're trying to fit in? We're trying to belong. But the truth is, when you're busy trying to fit in, you're not standing out.

That is worth repeating, "When you're busy trying to fit in, you're not standing out."

Dynamic Women™ stand out. They do. If you think of any woman who has inspired you, any woman with whom you wish you could be friends, with whom you want to do business, someone you're just watching as a leader in the community, and she's doing great things, being successful, she's happy in her life, that woman is standing out. She's unique in one-way or another. Right?

If you want more clients, more money, more freedom, more friends, and a man and all these other things, you need to stand out. I am not saying you need to be out there all crazy, and outgoing. Maybe that's not your personality, and I don't want you to change in that way. Instead, you are stepping into the authentic you. The real you. The unique you. Right? I said earlier in Dynamic You™, I'm not changing you as a person, but I want you to show up as the unique you.

Here's another question for you. Third question for the Dynamic You™ Global Community. What makes you unique? What makes you stand out? What is it? Don't just say, I'm tall or I've got red in the back of my hair. This isn't it. Maybe for me, I stand out because of my humor. I stand out because I talk with my arms. I stand out because I am loving. I stand out because I hug people. I stand out because I get excited about things. Because I am a leader. Because I am outspoken. What is it about you that makes you stand out?

If you're having trouble getting started, go back to the question of what makes you dynamic, and then ask other people. Be like, "Hey, friend. Hey, hubby. Hey whoever. Be honest with me. What makes me unique? What makes me stand out as different from everybody else?" I am excited to see these answers.

When Can You Be Real?

Now, in order for us to really tap into how it feels to be real, I want you to think about when you are with friends, family, your partner, other people who you're completely comfortable around. When you get to feel like yourself. Think of these moments. Are you thinking of a certain time? Do you remember some moment or can you think of people who you're around when you feel this way?

What does that feel like? What does it feel like to be truly yourself? Maybe it means you don't have to smile all the time. Maybe it means that if you're not happy, you can say it. Maybe it means you're not the 'hostess with the mostest' at every single second of every day so you actually get to sit and let others care for you.

I know that because I'm so comfortable around my husband and some of my friends, they hear everything in my mind. I'm in a place with these people where I don't need a filter. I'll just say things. And since I'm so comfortable sharing what I'm thinking and feeling, I assume they know everything that's in my mind. My husband said to me recently, "Honey, you didn't tell me that." I am so comfortable, I almost feel like I have told him everything and I don't even say everything because I feel like he already knows it. That's for me my ultimate level of comfort.

When I get around my girlfriends I can be silly and funny. I can be sarcastic, joking, and sometimes a little bit crude in how I am. In my videos I'm real. It is the real me. But I'm a little bit more animated than if we were sitting and having a coffee. Sometimes I'm a little bit more entertaining in how I speak and I change my voice, but that's because I'm fulfilling a job to deliver content to you that you're going to listen to. But I am still being the real me. I feel like I can do that, and that's why I don't mind if I have to scratch my face or if I stumble over my words, that's just who I am. I am not a perfectionist anymore. Anymore, right? Keyword anymore. I'm recovering.

In these moments, what does it feel like for you? And why is it better to be real than not real? I already talked about how it felt and all the negatives, but how does it feel when you're actually being real? I'll give you a few ideas.

Why It's Awesome Being Real!

1. **One, you get to be yourself.** Oh my gosh. How easy is it to be yourself? It should be really easy. You're in flow that way.

2. **It's automatic.** You don't think about it. You don't have to be wondering, "Oh my gosh, what do I think about this?" You don't need to think about how you should think, you just do it.

3. **Next, you don't overthink.** You don't have to be worried that "if I say this, they're going to think that." No, you just say it because it's who you are and you don't adjust who you are for anyone else.

4. If you're not in your head thinking about all this stuff, **you are actually present.** How amazing is that? The funny thing is, I said earlier that one reason why women are not real is that they feel more connected with people. So these women are saying what they think others want them to say, but actually, it's only a surface level connection. They may feel super connected to you, but you're not going to feel connected to them because they are not being themselves.

5. **You don't have to be "on".** What a relief! Being switched on all the time is emotional labour. I've felt that way teaching kids because it was an expectation of the company I worked for. Not having to do that brings the control back to you.

So, there are five reasons why it feels great to be real. I want you to really tap into those moments and those people in your life where you can be truly yourself.

Sometimes there can be the exception to the rule. Here's the disclaimer. Sometimes you need to put your best foot forward. And yes, there are times when you need to suck it up and fulfill a role or a job. You do not get to feel exactly how you want to feel or how you're being in that moment. For example, I lead Dynamic Women™ in Action events, and sometimes when I've led these I've had a headache, or something less than good has happened in my life and I'm distracted or not as peppy as usual. I'm guessing you can relate. Do you think I'm going to sit there and go, "Oh gosh, guys, I have the worst headache and I'm in a bad mood and this terrible thing happened to me?" No. I'm going to adjust my attitude. I'm going to say, "Hey, here we are and this is what we're doing." But I'm still acting like myself, I'm just not acting like myself when I'm 100%. Yes, you could say I'm kind of faking it, but I'm still the real me. I'm still being exactly how I would be if I were feeling my best. I am just, in that moment, not letting my emotions take over the objectives and intentions I set for that point in time. I have to be clear though, caring for yourself is important. And if you need to excuse yourself from doing something or be real about your situation, do that first.

Another example is from when I was leading a section of an event, I had a twenty-minute block of time to run these activities. By the end, only five minutes was left for me to do what I had spent a lot of time planning for. I was not happy with the situation; I felt that my value of commitment and fairness was dishonored. I was upset. But do you think I showed up pissed off, unorganized or unprofessional? No. I just rolled with it, and used that five minutes the best way I could. I simply chose not to show that any of it was an issue, and it actually ended up being a phenomenal experience. Not just for me, but for everybody attending. The cool thing is I was so real in that moment, people were running up to me afterwards. "Oh my gosh, Diane, I have to speak with you. I have to introduce myself. I had to know more about you." That's a moment where you realize, "Oh wow." I was so real in that moment, people connected with me. So I was actually lucky to have experienced that.

If you're thinking, "Well, no, Diane. When I go to these things, I can't tell them all my troubles." Well, no, you can't and you shouldn't. No one wants to hear you complain about everything in your life, and if you need to talk to someone, save it for those with whom you are closest. But you can still be you in spite of all your troubles. You just have a filter.

So, yes, sometimes you put on a happy face, but the point is that it's your happy face. Yes, sometimes you have to be professional, and sometimes you can't be your unfiltered self. I don't crack crude jokes in professional business meetings, just like I don't crack crude jokes around children. But it doesn't mean I am fake with either. I bring myself, my true self no matter where I am. Sometimes I am my kid-filtered self. Sometimes I am my professional self. When I'm speaking in public, I am my animated and entertaining self. Adapting our words and behaviors to be appropriate according to our audience and setting doesn't mean you are forsaking who you truly are. You are multifaceted and layered like an onion. And you have the power to choose which layer and how much of the real you certain people get to see in certain situations. You have the power.

Here is Your Challenge

Now let's get to your challenge. The challenge is for you to be the real you. No surprise. But I want to ask some questions to help you to be real.

First question is, where do you need to be honest about who you are? Which areas of your life? Which groups of friends? Are you acting a different way on a sports team, in a volunteer role, with certain people?

Next. I know we can all play different roles in different situations with different people. So, maybe one place you're a leader and another you're a follower, and here you're serious and there you're funny. I want to ask you what roles are you playing? Look to those different areas of your life, look to the different situations and all the roles you're playing and write them down. What are all the roles you're playing?

Now, I want you to choose what's your real way of being, on earth, as it relates to your purpose. What's your real role? I'm not saying you must use that as a blanket way of being. For example, "All the time I'm organized. All the time I'm serious." But, what is that ideal role that you will not play, but be? As a coach, I need to be curious all the time. I need to be in that coach mindset all the time. It's never, "Now I'm a coach. Now I'm not a coach."

Let me share a personal story with you. I was at a conference recently in Toronto, and when I approached the microphone to ask a question, I kind of stood back a little and stuttered "ummm." The woman on stage was a colleague of mine and knew I frequently speak in public. She said, ""Whoa, Diane, you're a speaker. Take that mic. Take ownership." And I thought, "Right. Yes. What am I doing right now? I'm being sloppy." I had to own it in that moment, and I appreciated her calling me out. That's what I do with my own clients. I call them out if they're not being their full selves and playing the wrong role.

What roles are you playing? What is the real role or ideal role you want to show up as?

Moving forward, I want you to be showing up as your authentic self, who you know yourself to be, in every situation and with all people. Trust me, you're going to rewrite the outcomes. Why? Because you are sharing the real you. You are going to speak up regarding what you want, rather than what other people want. You are going to be vulnerable, and that might be scary, but trust me, the freedom you'll experience when you can be yourself is all worth it. Remember, we're blowing past these boundaries because that's the only way we can step into our Dynamic selves. When you show up everywhere as the true you, the authentic you, the real you, it emphasizes what makes you different, what makes you unique. People will remember you. People will connect with you. People will think you are refreshing. And sometimes, you might need to speak your truth.

Pillar Two is be real. That's your challenge. Show up as the real you. And make sure you are spending time documenting this in your journal and with the Dynamic You™ Global Community. Tell us how it goes, because I want to know and so does everybody else. We want you to inspire us with what you say.

I encourage you to take a break from this book for a few days and implement the challenge to be real.

Pillar Two Check-in

How was being real? Compare your original feelings about the being real challenge with how you feel now, having completed the challenge. Any shifts? Anything else you noticed?

My client, *Claudine Pender*, shared, "I'm very honest and real, but I'm very self-conscious, so what's difficult for me is being comfortable being real. I want to be calmer inside when I'm being real."

Claudine was worried she needed to be 100% percent herself, and so she fully turned everything up while simultaneously being completely honest. That's a tall order. Being real doesn't mean you say everything that's on your mind all the time. It doesn't mean you have to be transparent with everyone in your life in all situations. You have the power to adjust the volume of your personality when necessary. You can opt to turn down certain aspects of yourself in order to be environmentally and audience appropriate. And when you feel like really shining, you can turn up your personality too.

Tazeem Jamal shared her experience after focusing on Pillar Two. "I go to prayers, and often times when I'm in my community, I'm really interested in the other women and ask about them. But when they ask about me, I'm quick to respond with a simple, 'Things are fantastic. Thank you!' and I put the focus back on them. But I noticed this week, after taking the challenge, when the women asked me how things are going, I actually stepped into it and told them about how I was speaking at an event and invited them to come. They were happy for me and started asking me more questions. I was feeling a little uncomfortable because of the attention, but it was actually kind of nice. One lady said she couldn't make it and wished she could support me, so [she] asked me how else could she do that. It was so nice for them to show interest, support me, and learn more about what I do. It helped me to have more common ground with them. I felt very real stepping into who I am."

How cool is it that when *Tazeem* was real, and shared more about herself, she was able to connect better with the women in her community and it boosted her confidence as well?

Being real provides opportunities, and Pillar Three is an example of just that.

Cora Naylor, "When have I not been the 'real' me? I tend to hide behind myself when meeting people in large groups. Whether for business or personal, I find it a lot easier to be myself meeting people in a one-on-one situation. I'm not a naturally outgoing type of person. If I go somewhere with someone that 'takes the lead,' I will fall back and go along. I don't feel that I'm necessarily putting on a 'fake' front, but I'm also not necessarily putting out my best self. What makes me 'standout?' I'm a good listener, trustworthy, and level headed."

Angela Foran, "I am usually the real me, but there are times when I hold myself back from saying or doing things that may be in conflict with others' beliefs. My uniqueness? This is a challenging one, but I'd say [I'm] adaptable, independent (I actually wanted to say not a team player but thought independent sounded more positive), adventurous, observant and compassionate."

Claudine Pender, "Why haven't I been real? I am real. Honesty is my biggest value. BUT, listening to Diane, I could think of a few instances. I heard all my life that I talk too much and I am too loud, etc. So, I try to be quiet. I wait until people speak first. It's not that I am not being real; I am waiting my turn. This is when I am in a group of people. I also feel very bad when people ask me questions and I talk non-stop and then I feel like I was the only one talking.

"Where am I not real? I am quieter in a large group of people (like in a conference) and I am not the one to raise my hand or volunteer, etc. Just because I want to let others, [who] are not so outspoken, have a chance. Instead of me 'taking their chances.' Ugh. I don't feel real with my step kids also, because I don't feel relaxed or part of the conversation. I feel I am always playing "catch up" with their conversation, so I smile and nod a lot.

"What makes me unique/stand out? I am kind. Really. I do my best to help everyone. I am FUNNY. I fought hard not to be funny, but it was so stressful and so tiring I finally accepted myself. I am VERY enthusiastic about stuff!!! Too much!!! I get really happy about what's going [on] with me and with others, and basically, I want to do everything!!!

"How does it feel to be real? I have great friends, and also, with my husband and my son I am very real. I don't have to measure my words. I can be funny and a bit CRUDE at times! I have some radical thoughts, that if you know me well, you understand! So I can share my radical thoughts... no fear of judgment. I am totally relaxed."

Sandra Girard, "When have I not been real? I think I am pretty real and authentic— what you see is what you get from me. I always try to show up as me and don't feel fake. At this point in my life, I find that it takes up too much energy not being real.

"What makes me stand out? I am friendly and enjoy connecting with people. I like to be engaged in many things, and [I] enjoy 'mentoring' women by sharing my stories and experiences. I feel powerful and energized when I feel real."

Claire Madin, "When have I not been real? I struggle to be real in new situations, such as a networking event when I do not know anyone, interviews when I let my nerves take over, [when I'm] new to an environment where I feel uncomfortable. I need to take time to assess who is who, and as I become more comfortable and familiar, I let the real me come in.

"Where am I putting on a fake front? I put on a fake front when I am not comfortable. In these situations, when I am nervous I will often let my saboteurs lead the dance. What makes me stand out? My Australian accent. Ability to connect with people. How does it feel being real? Relaxing, it does not take a lot of energy and is smooth. Where do you need to be honest about who you are? I need to be honest about who I am in my new work environment, so I can provide my clients with an amazing experience. I need to be honest at the gym and when in new networking situations. What roles are you playing? Roles include: fitness leader, friend, colleague, cheerleader for clients.

"My real role and my purpose being here is to be an advocate for women's fitness, building and developing a strong community for women to find time for themselves, indoors and outdoors."

Melody Owen, "I am myself most of the time. If people can't handle me, then we really aren't a match and that's okay. We are all good people, just not suited to each other. Where do I put on a fake front? That said, when I am in parent meetings or socializing with the parents of my children's friends, I don't feel that I can be truly myself. I learned early on as a parent that my children's social status and schooling depend on me fitting in. I try to avoid these settings as much as possible, and measure/protect myself (or my children) as much as I can when I must participate.

"What makes me stand out? I am very inclusive and see the humanity in the people I meet. I listen, really listen and observe, and I like to understand people. I often understand the unspoken in the conversations I have with others. I do not judge. I am good at connecting people and making everyone feel welcome. I am also able to be vulnerable and show my emotions, which I know makes some people uncomfortable. On the flip side, if you need someone to just sit with you while you weep, I'm that person. Another person's show of emotion allows us to see each other as human and I welcome it. When am I my true self? With my family, friends, out and about, networking, in business. Most of the time I am just me. I like me and like to spend time with the real me. I avoid situations where I feel the real me is unwelcome."

Leagh Wright, "I am always real and authentic. I pride myself on this and value it in others. I love sincere, truthful, and direct conversation. However, I feel I am not the real me in some ways. I have too much negativity and dysfunction in my life. I'm sensitive to negativity and dysfunction and it really clouds my sun. My potential and my greatness are compromised by this. I don't think I put on a fake front. For the most part, I don't care what people think. I think what makes me unique and stand out is my honesty, integrity, and openness. I also get through obstacles quickly; I don't dwell on things. What roles [do] I play? Leader, strong supporter, and comedian."

Chantal Staaf, "WOW Pillar One and Two were heavy duty for me anyway. Not that I am a fake person (one of the personality traits I quite dislike actually), but I do find at times I cannot be true to myself. I am a loud, happy, funny, animated woman. I enjoy a good time. I don't get embarrassed easily, but when I make an ass of myself, its cause I'm willing to do it for fun. I believe that life is much too quick to not have fun, be silly, and just be.

"There are definitely people I am not myself with; as I feel inferior, as though I can't bring info or worth to what I am saying. This gives me a very sad feeling. Unfortunately, I do feel some of this in my business. I also, in my family at times, feel this way, that my partner in crime is not on the same page. He is quiet when I get loud or excited, he almost gets pissed off.

"I remember once we went to a cheer comp and he sat there, clapped, and here's me whistling [and] freaking out about my 'baby' flying in the cheer routine. I understand it's not him to be loud, but the look of disgust on his face when I get out there excited makes me second-guess myself, and us, to be honest. When I go to a national conference, that's when I feel the real authentic self, I am me. I am real. I am successful and people KNOW me. That makes me feel like a million bucks. I dance with my friends, sing with the music, clap, and am loud. There is no judgment there. Perhaps, that is why I am having such a hard time with my business, taking a back seat. Perhaps, because it is clouding the true me? I do not know.

"I will remove my titles as a parent, dance and cheer mom, Epicure leader/consultant, Tim Horton's employee and I'm going to be me; loud, funny, touchy, feely me. It's going to be difficult, as I am so used to being defined by my role. This is very difficult for me divulge as it is making it very real. This morning I asked my oldest friends from over 25 years ago—what makes me unique? And this is what I got: Loyal, trustworthy, fair, compassionate, silly, delightful, witty, honest, hardworking. WOW!"

Pam Karlen, "I raise my hand to first four reasons why women are not 'real.' Thanks to coaching with Diane, I am beginning to step out and show the real me... to be DYNAMIC I wear a "mask" 50% of the time. It's one of those see-through ones with the painted face on it, so it's me, yet guarded. I wear it to fit in so I feel like I am connecting, and to protect myself of what others will think. Crazy, even with people I don't know and will probably not ever see again, and I only partially show myself to those close to me even. Rarely do I show the entire real me to anyone. I am getting better.

"What makes me unique? I'm excitable and heartfelt, meaning I wear most of my emotions on my sleeve. I'm fun-loving and can laugh at myself, shake it off and move on. I'm an explorer, I love to try new things, see from different 'eyes.' I'm inspirational/nurturer, animated, and can't sit still or be quiet for very long), honest, kind, caring, and I can go from one end of the deep, quiet [and] spiritually connected to the let's go have some crazy fun. I think my kids & grandkids call it embarrassing."

Fatima Sumar, "I forgot to answer two questions: Why do I act fake when I'm around my immediate family? Because I know I'm being judged when it comes to my finances. I act like everything is okay, but I'm far from it. I put on a fake front about things that matter to me, as I feel that no one will want to hear what I have to say or do."

Sukeina Jethabhai, "When am I not real? I think for the most part I am real and authentic. I don't think I've struggled with pretending to be someone or something I'm not. What I do struggle with is self-doubt post being authentic, if that makes sense. I'll approach every situation as myself, will for the most part speak my mind or be quiet and watch and then re think the situation to see if I acted appropriately or said anything that may have offended someone. In this quest to constantly re-think, I end up not trusting myself and berating myself after the fact if I think I said something wrong or made a mistake.

"What makes me unique? I am creative and have a good eye for design. I am helpful and enjoy putting together events, camps, retreats, and small group gatherings. I am a hard worker. How does it feel to be real? It feels good, although I think my self-doubt gets in the way."

Anneliese Dusseldorp, "I am stuck on Pillar Two, I know I'm not the real me at my 9-5 job, but I look at it as it pays the bills and that is it. Being in my business makes me happy and I can be the real me. I have struggled for a long time with what makes me . I have a big heart and am caring."

CHAPTER 4
PILLAR 3: CONNECTED

Are you ready for Pillar Three? Let's review the previous Pillars:
1. Pillar One: Dynamic Women™ Prioritize themselves.
2. Pillar Two: Dynamic Women™ are Real.
3. Pillar Three: Dynamic Women™ are Connected.

Women know a lot of people. Yes, we do. We like to chat with acquaintances, coworkers, friends, family, but are we truly connected to them? We know them, but are we connected?

What Does It Mean To Be Connected?

Let's first explore how Dynamic Women™ are connected. Dynamic Women™ connect with more people on a deeper level because they show up as who they are, the real them. They're not only connecting deeper because they show up as their authentic selves, the other person shows up too, both parties ignoring their titles and disregarding what they do. It's not that titles are inherently bad. They tell us who people are, yes. But the information they provide is only surface level and in a very specific context. What if those titles were irrelevant when we met each other? Can you imagine the possibilities then? If we want to connect on a deeper level, we need to use Pillar Three and connect as real, genuine people, forgetting titles and communicating as if there were none. We must be ourselves, turning up our good qualities and turning down the importance of our titles.

Think of it this way. When Shannon the Real Estate Agent meets Caryn the Lawyer, what reason is there for these ladies to connect deeply? Perhaps they would discuss the similarities and differences of their professions, but I can't imagine the conversation between these two producing much else. But if you put an interaction into deeper context and consider who each person truly is inside, it's the profound characteristics that will begin to guide the interaction, and we will find more and more reason to connect deeply. For example, instead of the case of Shannon the Real Estate Agent and Caryn the Lawyer, imagine a conversation between Shannon the great listener and well-organized woman and Caryn the funny and outgoing leader. Doesn't that sound like a much cooler conversation? Instead of Susan the Entrepreneur chatting up Henry the Contractor, we would say that Susan, who is passionate about life, is chatting up calm and collected Henry.

Connect On A Deeper Level

Focus on the other person. Don't focus on their title or their professional role. Don't focus on their level of achievement, or how far they are into their business. Don't focus on whether that person has kids or not, whether they can be labeled a mom or a dad. Or even if they're a dog owner. No. Strip the titles away, and you will unlock the opportunities you crave in order to connect deeply with more people.

> **Seek out strong women**
>
> **to befriend,**
>
> **to align yourself with,**
>
> **to learn from,**
>
> **to be inspired by,**
>
> **to collaborate with,**
>
> **to support, to be enlightened by.**
>
> **~ Madonna**

How Do I Connect This Way?

It may seem difficult at first, but don't worry. I'm now going to give you seven ways to help you connect deeper in any setting with anyone. Imagine yourself showing up to an event, a house party, at the gym, wherever you're going to come across people and have the opportunity to meet someone new. Study the list below, memorize it, or make flashcards, whatever you need to do. If you can internalize the following methods, you will find even more ways to truly and deeply connect with others.

1. **Connect with them based on emotion.** How she's feeling, positive or excitable, whatever it is.
2. **Connect with their experiences.** So, "She's someone who's also traveled from another country to live in this country."

3. **Connect with them based on likes.** "Oh, she likes spicy food too."

4. **Connect with them based on interests.** "Cool, she loves CrossFit and so do I."

5. **Connect based on struggles.** "Ah, she also has had children who XYZ." Or "We both have had companies close down and had to switch and go to a new one."

6. **Connect based on opportunities.** "Oh wow. She's a speaker and she's had this chance to go and do this and I want to do that, so I'm going to go talk to her about it."

7. **Connect based on desires.** "Both her and I have the same desire to give back to people in developing nations."

Can you already sense how much deeper and intimate your interactions are going to be if you use these methods? Which of the seven was most exciting or interesting to you?

A connection based on one or more of these factors is going to lead to a deeper connection. Once you make a connection, don't just stop there. Make it deeper. Get curious by asking more questions, like—

- "What's important about that for you?"
- "What part of it do you enjoy the most?"
- "What got you into it?"

The cool thing about this type of connection, this deeper connection, is that it crosses all demographics. Often instead of listening, learning, and deeply engaging in a conversation, we're so busy judging ourselves. We judge ourselves based on the fact we're not as successful as the person to whom we're talking. We're not as young as them, not as fit as them, not as rich as them, not as good a mom as them. Whatever stupid story you tell yourself, when you focus on titles and roles you're always going to lose because you become sick with "compare-itis." I've suffered from this disease before, and maybe you are now. The good news is that by training yourself to focus on the right things, you can be cured of it. Just remember that you and the other person are real people with real emotions, real feelings, and real struggles.

Connecting in this way crosses all demographics, so you don't have to worry about being excluded or excluding someone else. You can connect with anybody: male, female, young, old, successful or not, it doesn't matter. Because when you are in that place of "ah, we're both just people," you will be bolder, more confident, and more of the real you will show up.

I just watched a video of a woman in my Dynamic Women™ in Action community. This woman got the chance to meet one of her idols; i.e., the very woman who taught her how to do the work that she does in the world. She met her. What an amazing moment. For her, it was one of those "I met Oprah" moments. (And no, I haven't met Oprah, but it's on my list. So if you know her, tell her I want to connect and have coffee.) She shared in the video, "Oh my gosh, I met her and she was just a real person." Well, duh. Yeah. Famous people, rich people, successful people are just real people like you and me. Sometimes they say you shouldn't meet your idol or your hero because you'll be disappointed because you've put them on a pedestal and have such high expectations of them. But the woman I know was pleasantly surprised with meeting her idol, and that experience was shaped by the fact she showed up authentically, and she and her idol deeply connected based upon the work they do. This is a success story, because after studying and applying the Pillars, she seized the opportunity to meet her idol with the knowledge that she was a real person too, with real emotions, real feelings, and real struggles just like herself.

What's the expression? Everybody puts her pants on one leg at a time? Yeah. Everyone has trials. Everyone has weaknesses. Everyone succumbs to death and disease around them. Everybody deals with her own crap, basically. Once you realize, "I'm a real person. They're just a real person, and we can connect on a deeper level," you eventually shed all those false beliefs that limit and obstruct your way to making real connections.

Create Your Board

Dynamic Women™ don't merely make connections, they make the RIGHT connections. Key here is the word "RIGHT". This is crucial. Have you heard the Jim Rohn quote?

"You are the average of the five people you spend the most time with."

I love this one. I've taught this saying in Dynamic Women™ in Action, and I use it frequently with my clients. So now it's your turn. Name the five people with whom you spend the most time. Are they family? Colleagues? Up or downline? Clients? Friends? Write down their names. It could include your assistant, your nanny, your children, or even your boss.

If you were the average of those five people, what would be your level of success, positivity, ability, drive, leadership, etc.? Does that score excite you or scare you?

Now is the time you take control of your average score. You've named the people in your top five. Now, whom would you like to move into your top five? Let's create this like a board. If you were running your life as though it were an organization, a company or even a country, who would be the five people you'd hire to sit at that boardroom table with you each and every day? Unless you're spending a lot of time with them because you're a stay-at-home parent, it's not going to be your kids. And unless you do business with your spouse, don't include them in your top five either. We are talking about making relationships outside the normal ones we already have in our comfort zones. It doesn't have to be anyone you actually hang out with either. Maybe it's someone you're reading. Maybe you listen to podcasts and it's someone from whom you're learning. If you want to add me in, awesome. I would love that. Just know who you'd like your top five to be.

With my five people, I call them my team.

1. I have a Business Coach
2. A Numerologist
3. A strategist who's also a techy
4. A loving business owner and
5. A mentor in Licensing

Mine happen to be all female, but it's perfectly fine to have men in your top five if that works best for you. I did feel it was helpful for the people on my board to have successful businesses and children, because in the past few years, I too have been running businesses and growing my family. I wanted people on my board who would understand where I was coming from. I wanted people who could give me advice, and people who would know if my kids were a legitimate reason or if I was using them as an excuse. My top five are fantastic because they are like my supportive cheerleaders, pushing me to the next level. I can ask them questions and receive honest answers, and this helps me to be decisive. I can give you more examples of why they're helpful to me, my business, and my life, but basically, I wanted to show you the kinds of people you will want on your Team, on your board, in your top five, your Inner Circle.

You might hire some of them, trade with some. One person on your list may be a mentor of sorts. Some will help you more than you help them. Or maybe you will make an agreement to mutually support each other. In the case of mutual support, you will always move forward as a group. Because when you support each other and one of you succeeds, that success moves the other forward as well.

Let's get back to the fact that Dynamic Women™ have the right connections. Here are some key things I want you to write down. So, grab your journals. Don't forget you should be writing down most things, especially any questions I ask you and your answers.

Connect With The Right People

1. **Seek out more of the right people to connect with.** Be clear about who you are looking for, the qualities they should possess, and their purpose.

2. Once you know what you want, **let go of the people who aren't a great fit.** In your five, do you have someone bringing your score down? Someone who's usually negative? Get rid of them. Replace them. Remove them from your top five in a kind way. If they work for you, let them go. If they're a friend, spend less time with them. It's not that they're bad people, it's just that they belong on someone else's board. The longer you keep them on yours, the longer you are delaying their move to the right one. In the end, it will be better for both of you.

In the future when you're networking and you meet somebody who's not a good fit, don't ask for her business card. That way, there's no obligation for you to follow up with her. There's no need to say, "Hope to see you soon" or "we should have coffee". If you take her card and make empty statements when you didn't care for her, you aren't being authentic. Don't waste your time or hers. Instead say, "All the best," and focus on the people with whom you actually want to connect. I give you permission.

3. **Go out to places your ideal five hang out.** Go to those events, parties, conferences, check out your mutual connections through LinkedIn and Facebook, and just give them a call. When you attend events, look around the room to see if they are there. Even better, know who's attending an event before you go, so you know you will find the right people there.

4. When you meet people, **authentically connect with them on that deeper level**, and then ask yourself, "Is this the right person for me?" If they are, connect further. Call them, go for coffee, have strategy times,

invite them to events, send them interesting articles, quotes, videos and other things that will help form a deeper bond.

5. **Not everyone can be a fit.** Some people are meant to come into our lives for only a short while. Recently, I had someone come into my life who I felt wasn't very nice to me in an email she sent after coming to one of my events. I was shocked at first. But then I thought, "You know what? Bless her for sharing. She is being honest, and whether I agree with what she said or not, she shared."

Apparently, she felt she needed to teach me something. I listened. I took it for what it was. I blessed her and wished her all the best. She is not someone I will continue to be connecting with, but this is just how it goes sometimes. We learn from people and sometimes people learn from us. Who knows? Maybe she learned from me too. Maybe she just doesn't see it yet. The earlier you can decide whether or not someone will make a great friend or be mutually beneficial, the wiser the connection you make with them will be. If a relationship requires more work and energy than is necessary, don't waste your resources on that connection. Don't invest. Instead, spend your resources wisely on people who will return your investments.

6. **People will come into your five, and they will leave as well.** If you pay attention, you will find that most people fulfill a seven-year cycle in your life. They come in. There's some learning, some growing, some sharing, and then they move on. Maybe you have some people missing from your life right now, someone you think of and say to yourself, "Whoa, whatever happened to that person? We're not as close as we used to be." It could just be the seven-year cycle. Maybe her goals and intentions with you changed. The point is, relationships change and it's perfectly natural. The good thing is when you lose someone with whom you were close, someone who played an important role in your life, you're always going to find someone else. So the top five are not permanent. They continuously get replaced and replenished. If you're lucky, some people will stay on for a while and then just slide out to an outer circle, remaining easy to connect with.

I gave you a bunch of tips so let's recap.

1. Seek out people with whom you want to connect.
2. Let go of the people who aren't a fit.
3. Go find those who are.

4. Create a deeper connection
5. Know that people come into our lives to learn from us or to teach us something, and
6. There's a seven-year cycle on friends/connections.

Now It's Your Turn

I need to ask you the tough questions now. Who do you need to let go of in your life? In any area of your life, whom do you need to remove from your board? I want you to share on the Dynamic You™ Community. You don't have to share their name or who they are, but please share why you need to let go of them. Are they negative? Are they competing with you in a harmful way? Are they holding themselves back? Do they have terrible money stories? What is it about them? And why?

When *Fatima Sumar* reviewed her board, she realized she only had four people on it. And still, she needed to remove one of those because he was negative and bringing her down on purpose. After letting him go, she felt so much better, giving herself the opportunity to find great people to fill those two empty spots.

The second question is whom do you want to bring in? Whom are you seeking? What type of person do you need and why? Share it on the Facebook group as well. Those ones are awesome!

When *Pam Karlen* reviewed her five, she saw that she had been an introvert, too comfortable with being alone most of the time. After learning about having a board of five people, she has an opportunity to include champions and cheerleaders in her life and business and is excited about that.

Here Is Your Challenge

Are you ready for Pillar Three's challenge? Get excited because it's supported by Pillar Two, which trained you to be your real, authentic self. These are such complementary Pillars because being real creates a stronger connection. When you meet others, see them for who they are, not what they do, their titles or their roles. Ditch the titles. Take them out of that box, and look for the connection. That's your challenge. With everybody you meet, find the connection. Sometimes you might not be able to find it. But that's okay, you can always learn more about them in the time you have!

To take it up a notch. I like to do that, so I challenge you to see how fast you can find three things you have in common with this new person. Treat it like a game. Even if you're meeting someone while networking, grab her business card and write those things down on it. You will now have something better to talk about than just, "Let's talk about each other's businesses." Get creative. Be unique. Talk about something else, and let the professional aspect of that relationship blossom naturally.

While doing these two challenges, share your experience and its successes with the Facebook Community. Being a Dynamic Woman™ means so many different things, but these three Pillars are building the foundation for you to show up as who you want to be.

I'm looking forward to hearing all your stories. Please, share your obstacles. Share your struggles. Share your challenges. Ask your questions. Put your successes on the page from Pillars One through Three. As we keep adding, building one Pillar on top of the next all the way to nine, you can talk about any of the Pillars at any point. Please, just refer to them. "This is in relation to Pillar Two, about being real." This way, your fellow dynamic women get the context and you get to practice talking about the different Pillars.

My goal for you is to get the most out of this book, just like the ladies do in my program. I want you to really, fully step into the Dynamic You™, to be the woman you are meant to be.

Now is the time to take a few days focusing on Pillar Three. You can put the book down and pick up your journal to document how it's going and create your power board!

How Was The Challenge?

Pam Karlen, "I have been good about letting people and activities go that do not "fit" me any longer. I surround myself with people that are sincere and not only want to get but also give back "energy" (people who recharge me and I them). I try to avoid people who drain my energy. I study from people that have strengthen what I already believe. Who would I bring in? I would love to be a part of a small (3-4) "mastermind/soul" group who are all on a similar path of growing in business and personally."

Leagh Wright, "If I am the average of the 5 people I spend the most time with. That makes me alone. Which is accurate. I have outgrown some friends and have had a difficult time finding connections for the new and improved Leagh. People I've know for years can't believe the transformation. People I'm looking to connect with are conscious, ethical, supportive and intelligent. Thank you for your time ladies."

Angela Foran, "Right now I've got all good people in my life, so I'm keeping them all. I realized I don't meet a lot of new people and thought it might be good to expand my horizons a bit especially if I want to bring in a mentor or a collaborator. I'd like to have someone to bounce ideas off."

Sukeina Jethabhai, "I am strongly based in my community and most of my connections are from our mosque or religious affiliation. This is a double edge sword as I think sometimes the mindset can be limiting, but it's very comforting to have a supportive group who understands you culturally. I am seeking a broader tribe that is outside of my community. I really want to more intelligent women than myself. I think this will expand my mindset and help me grow more."

Melody Owen, "During today's call after my share I was thinking about connecting, giving and receiving, asking for support and giving support. The truth is they are all part of Pillar 3: Be Connected. So if I want to consider myself a good connector (And I do think I am a good connector!) then I must also be good at receiving and asking for support; not just giving."

"I like connecting with other people. I like people. Interestingly, this Pillar also opened up some challenges I still face. Who are my five people? 1. My Monday Business Nourishment group. (There are 5 of us in that group.) 2. Seth Godin - I don't know him but he is my favorite thought leader of our times along with Noam Chomsky. This question gave me good food for thought. I am going to make a list of thought leaders I would like to follow. Then I am going to read their books, watch their videos, and follow them on social media. Starting with Seth Godin who I already follow, I am going to check out Brene Brown, Zig Ziglar (Seth Godin talks about him!), Vala Afshar, Joe Pulizzi, Steve Buttry and Maria Popova.

"What type of person do I need and why? I need someone who is very supportive and encouraging. I have no family who talk to me unless they want something from me (other than my girls). This is very difficult for me as I am aware of the level of support a person needs for success especially as an entrepreneur.

"I have difficulty:

1. Believing I deserve support as I do not have family support and aren't they supposed to be the first place you go?

2. Understanding what support really looks like. Sometimes I question if I am actually getting support or not or if I just don't recognize support.

3. Believing that anyone would want to support me especially in the past few years when I have been feeling completely tapped

out and have nothing to give back to anyone. Hence, I never ask for support even though I would benefit from it greatly. I am not even sure what to ask, how to ask and what would be appropriate."

Sandra Girard, "Who do I need to let go of? I have let go of long time relationships that don't support me any longer. I find that I am now growing and stretching in so many areas of my life that I am having to revaluate what I bring to my relationships and what I need from them. People who are just fine with the way things are and take away my energy.

"Who do I want to bring in? I want to be surrounded by women who speak my language, that are inspiring and supportive. My skincare business is that tribe that inspires me and celebrates with me and encourages me to be better personally and in business.

Cora Naylor, "In the past few years I have made a number of changes in the people that I choose to be around, so I don't have anyone I need to let go of at this time. A few years ago I let go of a friend that I used to spend a lot of time with. We used to have a lot of fun together when we were doing the things she wanted to do, but when I started on my personal development journey the dynamics between us changed and I started going in a totally different direction. She wasn't really interested in what I was doing, so I made a decision to limit my time with her and now we never see each other... I think it's just like Diane said in the video - we were a seven year cycle friendship."

Comment from *Tazeem Jamal*, "Good for you Cora Naylor, it's NOT easy letting someone in your life go, but when you are both GROWING in different directions, it's makes for not so great conversations !!

Cora Naylor, "True... good news is there are lots of other people out there - just takes time to find the ones you click with."

Comment from *Claudine Pender*, "Thank you for sharing, Cora Naylor! Congratulations on being strong enough to set your boundaries with this friend. I have a hard time letting go of people."

Comment from *Sandra Girard*, "WOW Cora, your story sounds so familiar. I have needed to play in a new "sandbox" for a while and felt some of the relationships I had were not growing and stretching with me. I have let go of two 25+ year friendships over the past two years. I actually felt so much lighter! We are in people's lives for the time and reason we need to be. I loved those friends in my love at the time they were. It just doesn't fit now and that's OK

CHAPTER 5
PILLAR 4: PERSPECTIVE

How Far Have You Come?

If you have been stepping away from the book, then you read Pillar One a couple of weeks ago. What did Pillar One tell you to do? Prioritize yourself. Yes! Dynamic Women™ prioritize themselves so that they amass the resources and energy to take care of everybody else. You might have found that in prioritizing yourself, you have to say no to other things, and that's okay. That is totally fine because that's how you'll fill your cup, it will actually overflow, and there will be more bounty for everybody else.

Pillar Two is about being real. Yes, be authentic. Be yourself. That does not mean divulging every single secret you keep, and it does not mean being your full, complete, awesome, and quirky self in every single situation. You're still going to decide when it's appropriate and when it's not, and how much of that 100% other people get to see.

In Pillar Three, you learned about connecting to other people on a deeper level because Dynamic Women™ don't merely connect on the surface. They build relationships by stripping away titles, showing up as more than just their labels and roles, but as themselves. They profoundly connect with people, and then they look for people to fill their board. Remember Jim Rohn's quote about being the average of the five people with whom you spend the most time? Dynamic Women™ are filling those five spots with the right people at the right time, and that means people rotate in and out. So change them out. Switch them out for others.

Now, before I get to Pillar Four, I just want to say, I am so proud of you for reading this and for continuing on this journey. I know you are going to step fully into being the Dynamic You™ that you are, and you will create amazing results from this program. And so with Pillar Four, we're getting pretty close to that halfway point.

Pillar Four is Perspective

Dynamic Women™ use Perspective. Perspective is how we view something. It's your point of view. It can also be seeing things from a different angle and putting ourselves in another's shoes.

Let's try something. What are you working on right now? Is there a project with an approaching due date? Is there something that is kind of looming over you?

For me, I was recently having a new banner made. I wanted one of those photography banners that hang behind people so that when you take photos of them in front of it, the names of sponsors and other important things are displayed in the background. My banner was going to read, 'Diane Rolston' and 'Dynamic Women™ in Action'. The only problem was I had a very short window of time to accomplish it. Basically, I decided to start it a mere 24 hours before I needed it, showcasing it at an event of mine called Dynamic Celebration™. I had given myself such a short deadline, and it was difficult to not adopt a perspective that said, "I have no time to get this done. This is not going to happen. There's no point in trying!"

That was the perspective I held until I called my print broker and found out the banner could be accomplished as long as the graphics were completed by a specific time. My perspective went from "it's impossible" to "it's doable". My perspective could have been, "It's doable, but it's a crunch, and I don't think the timing will work," but my perspective was, "I'm going to make this happen because I really want it, and so it's doable within the time that I have. I only need the right people to make it happen." I needed to get my graphic designer on board, and I needed her to clear her schedule. The way I showed up influenced her. My attitude helped her decide she wanted to be part of it and that she could get it done on time. If I had come to her stressed out and with the wrong perspective feeding my attitude, she could have decided she didn't have the time. So when we look at all the possible perspectives, you can see how some served me well and how others would have been disadvantageous.

I want you to think of that project or that thing you're working on right now, what is your perspective of it?

If we put that topic/item/situation/person in front of you (for me, it was making that banner) what's your perspective on it? What are your thoughts? What point of view are you taking? What angle are you looking at it with? Okay, so just hold onto that point of view because I'm going to explain a little bit more about perspective.

You know your perspective. Now what happens if you have the wrong perspective? As you saw in my example, I could have just not even attempted the banner; I could have given up. I could've been a victim of circumstance saying, "Oh, there's just not enough time, so I can't get it done." There were so many different obstacles and negative results that could have happened, but instead of focusing on the negative or using the wrong perspective, I focused on using the best perspective.

I'll give you a bunch of reasons why this Pillar, of using your Perspective, is fantastic. Just so you know, perspective is something I do with my clients all the time, so you're getting one of my tools here out of my toolkit. I often say to my clients, can we change your perspective here?

Let me just share exactly how Dynamic Women™ use it. When they realize that they're looking at things through a certain perspective that is wrong for them, they say, "Okay, this one's not serving me, so I need to change it." Or "This one is not helping me, so I need to adjust it, and try a different perspective on."

Taking on a project with someone when you have conflicting perspectives is frustrating. If you've ever faced someone who has one narrow way of looking at the world, you know how impossible it can seem to try to get them to change their point of view. You tell them they're not seeing the whole picture. You tell them how much better off they would be if they looked at it a little differently. I'm sure there have been times in your life when someone else has helped you with your own perspective. Maybe you were feeling depressed and negative, and a friend helped you see the bright side of things. If you hadn't talked to your friend and bounced your ideas off them, you wouldn't have known a better perspective existed. If you don't talk to other people, then you don't get to see what else is possible. Let me tell you five reasons why using perspective in the right way is imperative.

Five Reasons to Use Perspective

1. New Opportunities

Having the right perspective can bring new opportunities your way. I received an e-mail from a client of mine who wanted to apply to a conference as a workshop leader. My perspective was, "I'm supporting her in this. She has a deadline today to get this in." I didn't at all think about this as an opportunity for myself. But then she wrote, "Hey, maybe you should apply too." Ah-ha. Maybe I should! And then I thought, this is so crazy that I'm going to whip up an application in a couple of hours to be a workshop facilitator and fly down to this conference in the states. Why don't I instead apply to be their keynote?

My perspective changed from, "The conference is too far away. And it's my client's opportunity" to "I've got nothing to lose here" and so I went for it. And what happened? Well, I'm happy to say that I was chosen as their keynote. Whoop! Whoop! Thanks to the little nudge from my client, I encountered a new opportunity because my perspective changed.

2. Increases Your Motivation

Think of someone who annoys you or keeps asking for stuff, and you don't want to help them. Instead of "I don't want to do that," maybe you switch your perspective to, "You know what? It's good karma if I do it, or maybe she knows somebody that she'll refer me to." You just look at it from a different point of view, and then you may feel, "Okay, now I want to do this" and so your motivation increases.

3. Makes You More Positive and Grateful

Maybe you've experienced this yourself. Say you're working at a 9 to 5 job and you want to be doing a side business or another type of business or just a different job instead. You may resent the job you have. If you consider that job as the item, and you ask yourself "what's my perspective on it?" you will conclude, "I resent it" or "I hate it. It might just suck the life out of me because this is not what I should be doing. This sucks. This is terrible. I don't want to do this."

Switch your perspective to, "You know what? This is paying my bills. This is allowing me to do my business on the side. This is allowing me to do my business and not take clients I don't want to take. This is allowing me to go to school or to pay for this for my kids." You can see how altering your perspective helps you be more positive and grateful. The things you thought were sucking the life out of you are suddenly giving you something for which to be grateful.

4. Allows You To See New Possibilities and Change

I'll give another example from my life. Identifying my house as the item, my perspective of my house was that I viewed it as a starter home, and if you know the Vancouver (BC, Canada) market, you know that housing prices are extremely high. When my husband and I moved here, we bought a townhouse, which at the time was bigger than we needed as a young couple with no pets. Since townhouses were worth between $700-900,000 CAD, and detached homes were between $1 and $2 million CAD, we decided we'd use the townhouse as our starter home before moving into a detached house. After a cat and two kids, we felt it was time to move into a detached house, and so instead of loving my home, my perspective was still, "This is only a transition house and I don't love it because it's not a detached home." I had missed out on many years of joy in this home because of that perspective.

When I changed my perspective from, "This is my home right now until we go and buy that larger home, that dream house" to "This is a great home for us and I'm grateful that we can even have a home in this market," I started to see the possibilities in my home. This new perspective helped me to see I could change things, and so what did I change? Well, we are redecorating for us rather than for resale. We recently put new floors in, new windows, repainted, and bought some new furniture. I thought, "I need to just put some love back into this home," and so I saw the possibilities, yes, but I also I became more grateful (reason 3), and it increased my motivation (reason 2).

5. Will Make You More Resourceful and More In Control

I mentioned before that you can feel like the victim of your circumstance, if you're looking at whatever the situation is and resigning yourself to thoughts like, "this is how it is" and "I don't like this, and this is negatively affecting me." But if you decide to adopt the right perspective, your thoughts will sound like this. "Okay, well, if I choose a different perspective here, then I'm now choosing how I feel about it. I'm choosing to make the change of how I see this thing." And with your new perspective you can ask yourself, "What resources are possible, are here for me?"

As you know, Dynamic You™ started as a program, but originally it was meant to be only a book. My feelings about writing the book were that it was a process I would undergo alone. As much as the book resonated with me, I didn't like it as much when I was doing it alone. I felt like I was pushing. Writing a book wasn't as easy as I thought. And so I considered a different perspective. What if I focused on when I'm my most brilliant and engaged my community? I was willing to give this new perspective a try.

I had to first sit in that perspective to figure out what it would mean and what it would look like. How can this still be my coaching and my teaching but involve others? How do I write a book that isn't only me writing alone, or just sitting and typing? How do I make writing a book a collaborative experience? After enough thinking, I was able to make the switch. It wasn't a book I was writing; it was a program I was capturing in a book. It allowed me to fully engage my skills, to connect with real women in real time and see their responses, answer their questions, and coach them through the process LIVE. I love the program and so do the ladies, and I trust you're loving it in its book form because you're still reading.

It comes back to you. Where do you need to change your perspective? Which areas of your life? Go back to that Wheel of Life with all the areas. Which area do you need to change your perspective? Is it around money? Is it around your spouse? Is it around your friends? Put that thing in front of you, and then ask yourself, what is my perspective? What is my perspective of my career? What is my perspective about my home? What is my perspective about my personal development? My perspective of fun and recreation? And so on. You might hear limiting beliefs coming out. "Fun and recreation! There's just not enough time for it." That's not a great perspective. You need to change that. Figure out where you need to change your perspective, which area, or with which person or project or whatever it is.

Here Is Your Challenge

You actually have two challenges for this Pillar. The first challenge is to look at all those places you need to make a change and choose at least one in which you will make a perspective shift. At least one, okay? Then let us know how it goes. For example, if it was, "My perspective of my husband is that he's lazy, and he doesn't help out around the house" What could be a new perspective? "I'm grateful he works hard at his job and that he earns money for our family," or "He's an amazing dad." Wouldn't that be a much better perspective to have? He's an amazing dad rather than he's a lazy husband. Of course!

Think of other things like your job. As I said before, it could be "This job sucks because it's not what I really want to do," and change that to, "This job allows me to have stability and to travel," or "My job allows me to get paid and do my side business," whatever your perspective is make sure it is serving you.

Challenge number one is goal-based, so you're going to make one perspective shift. Then you also have a process-based challenge, because I don't want you to just make that shift and that be it. Instead, what I'd love for you do is to look at your life throughout the day, as you're going through life, stop and think:

- What perspective am I holding right now?
- Is it serving me?
- What different perspective could I hold?

If you're in a situation like a meeting, and your perspective is, "This meeting is boring. All I want to do is go eat lunch." The perspective you're holding is, "This is a waste of time." Change your perspective to, "This is going to give me lots of new opportunities," and then you'll find that your intention switches. Your mindset will also shift. So you have a process and a goal-based challenge with this Pillar, and I know you're going to do a great job.

How Was The Challenge?

Fatima Sumar shared how she used to think the other people in her family weren't pulling their weight around the house. And now through her new perspective she sees everyone doing his or her part. When I asked, "How does this new perspective feel?" *Fatima* shared, "I feel like the bricks have been taken off my shoulders. I feel lighter."

Angela Foran shared she didn't realize she was even looking through any particular perspective at all. Instead, she just thought she was into the habit of thinking negatively and that she should change that bad habit and think positively. Learning Pillar Four gave *Angela* the vocabulary to talk about the things she was already doing, and provided new ways to think about these mechanisms. Using this Pillar in many areas of her life, *Angela* now sees how it will especially help with finances. Her usual perspective was either, "There's not enough money" or "there's lots right now." When she felt like there was plenty, she spent above her means and then would feel guilty about it. When we were coaching on some new perspectives, she said, "In the past, I didn't worry much about [money.] But as I get older, I worry more because my husband wants [more] security and it is rubbing off on me." So, "Money brings security" became her new perspective regarding her financial life.

Then *Claudine* shared, "I don't want to be old and poor" was her perspective.

Other points of view are,

- "There's more than enough"
- "Money is just a tool"
- "Money comes easily and flows abundantly"
- "I trust that I have everything I need right now"
- "Money is a vehicle to provide options"

Claudine originally chose, "There's more than enough," but she didn't really believe it deep down. So then we chose, "Money is just a tool." She believes that more, and likes how it confirms that she can achieve whatever she set her sights on. This perspective resonates with her because she is currently saving for a trip, and so she is living with this perspective in mind, viewing money as a vehicle for the trip.

"Once you shift the perspective, figure out how you are going to lock it in. You can do this through Yes/No Statements. For example, with the money perspective you could use, "I'm saying yes to creating a budget." For eating healthy, "I'm saying no to eating packaged food." You will create three of each." This will help you be more decisive, and you'll have confidence in your perspective. They are not just affirmations. Make sure you believe each one and that they resonate with you.

Here are *Angela's* Yes/No Statements:

1. I'm saying yes to opportunities to grow my business
2. I'm saying yes to saving money with purpose
3. I'm saying yes to hiring help in my business
4. I'm saying no to spending that is not a necessary business expense
5. I'm saying no to continuing education that is not related to my area of focus.
6. I'm saying no to scarcity mentality

As much as *Sandra Girard* would say she is usually successful in keeping her perspective positive, she often gets "emotionally charged". "My husband is good at calling me out and helps me see that it really isn't that big of a deal. By changing my perspective, I am able to look at the positive side of things instead of 'what went wrong.' It's important to remember not to let the negative things drain your positive energy."

Why would I be sharing the personal stories of these women with you? Well, Pillar Four is about changing perspective, and stories are the most powerful way to do that. You may naturally forget a lot of what you read in this book. You may have to read some things over again, but you will always remember the personal stories. Humankind has an affinity for stories. We've been telling them since our beginning, long before stories could be recorded with the written word. We remember stories, their beginnings and their endings better than anything else. These women's stories are a gift to you because when we read stories that resemble ours, and those stories end with success, we can't help but to feel inspired. If you haven't done so already, I urge you to log onto the Facebook page, and if you don't feel comfortable sharing anything yourself, at least read the comments from other women. Learn of their struggles. Know their accomplishments. I promise you, it will help you change your perspective, your perspective of your life, of your story, of yourself and your journey here.

Let's read a few more.

Angela Foran. "I started a regular meditation practice about four years ago, which has helped me with my perspective of different areas of my life, especially with regards to family interactions and health. With business, I find it more challenging [and] I resist a fresh perspective, maybe because I'm happy with where I am or maybe because I don't have a clear vision of where I want to be going or the areas I think I need to work on in my business aren't my strengths. I am very open to trying new things when I see there is a problem."

Claire Madin. "Perspective can be everything, it can hold me back and have a significant impact on those around me as well. I aim to be positive, this is something I have worked on. One thing I do is when my husband and I come home from work or are in a cranky mood from work or life, we call each other out. This is a great way to take a moment, become aware of your mindset and choose to share, clear or change to a positive perspective. The perspective I hold right now is I am so excited to be heading to the Dynamic Women™ Celebration Night, my dress is on and I look forward to seeing everybody. I could also be nervous, as I am giving a speech, but no, I am looking at this as an amazing opportunity to share my journey with amazing like-minded women!"

Chantal Staff. "I am good at 'preaching' about this. I am always the making-lemonade-out-of-lemons kinda gal. However, I have been feeling yucky lately and having a hard time bringing myself out of it. Seeing things VERY blue instead of the rainbow I usually see. SO my talent for changing perspective needs some work for sure. I will also be embracing this challenge. This Pillar has for sure spoken to me."

Melody Owen. "I am an open-minded, positive person. I tend to be able to look at a situation without judgment, just to observe, and I find this helps me take a situation and roll it around like a ball in my hands, seeing it from a number of different angles. That [being] said, I find I must remind myself that I need to ask, 'What can I do?' rather than say 'I can't.' Because I have too many responsibilities. I don't have enough time. I have limited resources, etc. I need to remind myself that I am one person and that as long as I am moving forward, I'll get there (wherever that is!) one day."

CHAPTER 6
PILLAR 5: SELF-AWARE

Pillar Five is about being self-aware. Are you aware of what you're thinking right now? How are you feeling at this exact moment? Tired? Happy? Curious? What's the feeling? What are your thoughts? What's your perspective right now? Think about your answers to each of these questions. I'm going to explain a little bit more about what it means to be self-aware.

What Is Being Self-Aware?

When you are self-aware, you know your own character, your own personality. It includes your strengths, your weaknesses, your thoughts, your beliefs, your feelings, your motivation for doing things, and your desires. It's as if we could take a special mirror and hold that mirror up and see what's going on inside of us. You're looking inward at yourself. Knowing clearly what exactly is on the inside is what it means to be self-aware. When we're self-aware we examine our current behaviors, thoughts, feelings, and way of being, and we compare those things to our standards and values, how we want to be. Being self-aware is how we become the best and fullest version of ourselves.

Dynamic Women™ know the many benefits that come from being self-aware. Basically, when you meet a Dynamic Woman™, you feel like she says the right things or she is confident. When you're around her and she is talking and doing things, you think, "Wow, she emanates a lot of success and positivity and happiness, and everything is all moving along in the right way for her." Everything's lined up. Everything's in tune.

I'll give you five very specific benefits to being more self-aware. But first, be self-aware right now. What are you thinking about? What are your thoughts? What are your behaviors? What are your actions? What are some of your strengths and weaknesses at this exact moment? I'm going to keep asking you these questions because there are always new things to learn about ourselves. So are your answers different from a few moments ago? By being aware of yourself, have you changed in any way? This is the power of being so in tune with ourselves.

Five Benefits Of Being Self-Aware

1. Your Judge Yourself Less

I know from all the clients I've talked to that self-judgment is the hardest for women; we are so good at judging ourselves. I shouldn't speak for everybody, but I know that even when I finish a task and I did a great job, I still make a list of things I would do differently next time. But when we become self-aware, we get to stop comparing ourselves to others because we're only comparing ourselves against our own standards. The dialogue would be, "Okay, in that situation, I didn't think or act or behave or feel the way I want, so next time I will intentionally do it differently." It's based on what you want, not what everyone else wants. As long as your standards aren't ridiculously high or out of line with your values, then you're good.

2. We Further Utilize Our Abilities

Yeah! Instead of thinking about our flaws, what we are good at and what we aren't simply becomes facts rather than judgments. We can ask ourselves, "What is this telling me?" And the answer should be, "Okay, so I'm not really good at these things, what do I want to do about it?" You have a choice.

You can improve if you want to, seeking opportunities to perform better. Or you can connect with the five on your board. You should have people on your board who live up to the standards you set for yourself, that way you can learn from them, absorb their techniques, get better alongside them. And you hire people to work for you, hire people who are good at the things you're not. Make things a little easier on yourself by having a team of people who are capable of taking care of you too. By having team members who do some things better than you, the very things you're not particularly good at, you allow yourself to let go of all the guilt and pressure. You free yourself and your time to concentrate on the things at which you excel. In this light, you're utilizing your abilities more because you're able to focus on the skills and talents you possess, rather than all the things you don't. There's no self-judgment. You save energy and get more done.

3. You Make Room For Change and Resetting The Course

This awareness gives you the ability to make changes in your life that will improve everything. You'll start hearing yourself say,

- "Okay, I don't like this way of being."
- "I don't like this thought."
- "This isn't the standard of behavior I want to put forward."
- "This isn't how I want to show up in this situation."

Then you'll correct your course. Just like a plane flies with navigation tools, self-awareness is a part of our navigation system. We will know if we're off course, and by making small adjustments we will end up at the right destination.

When you are able to be self-aware and know what's happening inside and out, then you are able to make changes and improve your life. Over time, with improved self-awareness, you won't only make changes after something goes wrong. But as you become better at it, you'll start to see warning signs and triggers as they come along, and when you see those signs, you'll make a change sooner rather than later. Instead of waiting until something goes wrong and having to fix it in the aftermath, you'll have already read the signs and made the necessary changes. For example, you know how to read your kids. You know the signs when your kids are hungry, and you know how to handle the situation before it turns ugly. You don't wait for your kids to starve or have a meltdown before feeding them, you recognize the signs as they come and find a solution before it reaches the boiling point.

Being self-aware and catching behavior early also means you can adjust things in advance. For example, if you need to go to an event, but you're already in a bad mood or feeling tired, you know you need to either do something to feel better or make changes to accommodate it. So a quick nap, or some healthy foods, or inviting a friend to come with you might lift you up. Or if you can't get yourself in an ideal mood, you may opt to arrive right on time or a little later and leave as soon as it ends. Or maybe you'll simply expect less of yourself and not force unnecessary networking. You can change things in advance rather than allowing the entire event to be a waste and having a terrible time forcing your way through it.

4. Improves Your Ability To Manage Emotions

When you're aware of your thoughts, your interpretations, and your perspective, you're able to tune into your emotions and move through them faster. Emotions exist to provide you with information regarding yourself or a situation. So if you're a good listener, you can hear those emotions out, assess them thoroughly and learn from them. Those feelings will flow through you quicker because you are able to provide yourself with what you need in order to move on and feel the way you'd like.

For example, if you're feeling scared about a presentation, your emotions are telling you that you care about doing a good job. You care about what you are going to say and you want your audience to make a change. Once you are self-aware enough to listen to that emotion, you can then focus on satisfying those objectives rather than just feeling fear.

Improving how we manage our emotions helps us to make good decisions. For instance, if you're hiring someone new you can listen to your emotions for information about that person. Does it feel right talking to them? Or do they make you feel uneasy? Trusting our gut, observing our emotions, and listening to our intuition are all part of being self-aware.

5. Improves Your Perspective And Where You Focus

This is how it works. Targeting all aspects of self-awareness—your thoughts, beliefs, attitudes, and actions—improves your life because you focus on the things you truly want. You make changes for the better because whatever you focus on becomes your reality. If you're focusing on having a better mood, positive thoughts, kinder actions, and greater results, then your reality will become those things. Your reality will improve because you're focusing on the right things, rather than things that drain your energy and knock you out of the flow. Being self-aware is maintaining focus on the things that will help you to attain a higher level of living.

Dynamic Women™ are self-aware, and the interesting thing is that when they are self-aware, they're also aware of how others view them. It's again, like the mirror. We put it up to see how others see us. Now, one way to find out how others see you is to ask them. Make a coffee date, pick up the phone, or even send them a survey. Another way of seeing yourself differently is to videotape yourself talking, watch yourself, and ask yourself these questions:

- What do I think about this person?
- If I just saw this person for the first time what would I say about them?
- Am I showing up in a way that I want?
- Is it according to my standards and values?
- Am I really connecting with others?
- Getting back to the other Pillars. Am I real? Am I connecting?

This is going to be a little bit like Pillar Four regarding perspective. In this challenge, I want you to set an alarm every hour, whether on your phone or an alarm clock or the oven timer, whatever you want. Set an alarm for 60 minutes, and when it goes off, take note of your thoughts, your emotions, your words, and your behaviors for the last hour. You are practicing self-awareness.

When the alarm goes off you are going to ask yourself these questions:
- What are my current thoughts?
- What are my current emotions?
- What are my current words?
- What are my current behaviors?

Check yourself and see if you honored your values and standards over each hour. If you do, then great! Pat yourself on the back. High five yourself, whatever you need to do and continue doing that. If you didn't, and you say to yourself, "I was being grouchy" or "I'm not doing a good job" or "I'm judging myself," whatever it is, write it down. Then, say to yourself, "okay, that's not how I want to be. That's not how I want to act," and make a change in that moment. Just try again and try harder for the next hour you set the alarm.

If you want to set the alarm for every 60 minutes and then every 45 minutes, and then every two hours, that's fine. I've had clients start with five minutes of every hour, so if they worked 55 minutes, they use the last five or the first five minutes of the next hour to examine themselves, ask those questions, and practice self-awareness. Whichever way you want to do it throughout your day, the intention is that you do it. At least eight to ten times a day, set an alarm to go off and ask yourself the tough questions. . .

For the doers (people who like lists and checking things off) this might feel like a waste of time. But if you don't stop to check in with yourself, you can mistakenly make quick decisions that may not be the right choice for you. But being in the moment and practicing self-awareness allows you to observe your emotions and mental state, examine what you feel like doing and what you don't feel like doing. Ultimately, you'll be more in tune with yourself to complete any activity.

Let's practice, what are your feelings and thoughts and emotions and actions right now compared to when you started reading Pillar Five?

Take this challenge and go out into the world and be the Dynamic You™ that I know you can be. It has been such a joy going along this journey with you. I look forward to chatting with you on our Dynamic You™ Global Community. Ask me a question, share a challenge, whatever it is, whatever's come up for you around these Pillars or our previous Pillars.

This is an opportunity and Dynamic Women™ take opportunities. Dynamic Women™ put themselves out there. Dynamic women stretch out of that box they've put themselves in so that they can grow and grow and grow.

In life, you must seize opportunities, because if you don't, somebody else will. Just like this ad from a major retailer I saw where the ladies had found the ultimate dress or shoes or handbag, but didn't buy them, so they were devastated when they found the item was gone when they went back to pick it up. Have you seen that ad or had a similar experience? I don't want you to feel like you've missed out on anything here. I want you to capture these opportunities. We are almost halfway through the Pillars, so let's step it up, let's step in, lean in, and get the most out of this book. Take a few days to implement this challenge and share how it went.

How Was The Challenge?

In a group call for my Dynamic You™ Program, *Pam Karlen* admitted that she didn't set an alarm and practice self-awareness. She later said she probably would have benefitted from it, and so she has now recommitted to doing it.

Melody Owen shared that setting the hourly alarm interrupted her work flow, so instead, she did it as a transition between activities. She doesn't like being disturbed when she's in the middle of a task, so this was a better system for her. She is working on having that break time. It helped her to see how the last task felt for her, so she knew what she needed to do next time in order to be more productive at those moments.

Angela Foran let us know that for a while now she has also been randomly checking in with herself. "At any moment a thought will pop into my head, 'I feel ___, [or I'll ask myself] how do I feel?" I sometimes will delve deeper and ask why [questions,] but now I have been incorporating 'what do I need?' which I really like. And I have been trying to take notes of the time and what I am doing to see any patterns I may have."

If you like *Melody* and *Angela's* approach to checking in throughout the day during transitions between tasks, then ask yourself how many times you will check in a day. When you do, write a few words down each time so you can start to see patterns and remember what you're feeling and thinking.

Melody did confess though that she's definitely a work in progress. She's right! We are all constantly growing and going through the stages of change.

The Five Stages of Change Model

1. Pre-contemplation
Either you don't know you have a problem or you deny/avoid it. The denial happens because you don't believe you can do it, you don't feel you need it or you don't want the discomfort.

2. Contemplation
You know you have a problem and you're weighing out the costs and benefits to see if it's worth doing something about it.

3. Preparation
If you're here you have decided to make a change within a month, and you are taking steps to make it happen.

4. Action
You are working on changing and putting new behaviors, thoughts, etc., into action.

5. Maintenance
You have successfully made the lifestyle change and no longer have the problem. It is a way of life and comes naturally to you now.

If you don't feel ready to do something, then ask yourself what you need and which Stage of Change you are in.

Claudine shared that she was grateful for this Pillar because when she took a moment to check in with how she was feeling, she realized she was sad her son was moving out because it was two years earlier than he said he would. When I asked her about it, she said, "You helped me a lot. Being self-aware helped me to change my perspective. Then when you asked what are you celebrating? I said, 'I'm going to celebrate him being healthy and independent.' Being self-aware showed me how it took over my feelings and my focus, but when I checked in with how I was feeling, I was able to change my perspective as well. It also helped me to then reach out to others and hear about their perspective and how they dealt with things, so I knew that I'd survive."

Sukeina found she used self-awareness in both positive and negative ways. When she uses self-awareness positively, she wakes up and checks in with how she is feeling. Throughout the day she checks in to see if she is tired, how her energy and mood is, etc. However, when she negatively uses self-awareness she checks in and ends up judging herself, feeling guilty for having the feelings she has.

But the truth is, there's no room in self-awareness for judgment. When you are self-aware, you are simply taking inventory of your inner world and acknowledging those facts, not making judgements about them. For example, "it's a fact I was feeling lazy and grouchy." Acknowledge that fact and stop there. Don't go on to judge that fact. Don't decide that feeling lazy is a bad thing. Just allow yourself to recognize that you were in fact feeling lazy, no more and no less.

If you do find you had feelings unaligned with your standards, or you acted in a way that does not reflect your values, ask yourself, What do I need? So you might have felt a little frustrated or snippy to someone. What do you think you needed?

- Food
- Space
- A break
- Sleep
- To do a different activity/task
- To talk it through

I know I get "hangry" (angry because I'm hungry) when I need to eat. Instead of judging myself for getting in a little mood, I show myself compassion and feed the solution, not a judgment regarding the problem. If we don't give ourselves a moment to be self-aware, then we don't respect our emotions. We rob ourselves of the time we need to process what we're feeling.

For example, in the morning when my kids would wake me up screaming, "Can we watch TV?" I hated it, and I knew I didn't dislike my kids, I just needed to be woken up in a different way. I wasn't angry at myself for not loving my kids all the time, instead, I decided to get up earlier by setting my alarm, which wakes me up with a lovely chiming sound. I could then stretch in bed, wake myself up calmly, and be ready for whatever form my kids would be in when they'd come running, excited to be awake.

Ideally, you arrive to the place *Claire Madin* is in. She shared how being self-aware has helped her to save energy and work more efficiently. Because she cares about her own needs, she can be decisive, knowing how she feels about different things throughout her day.

"This really is a pivotal one for me! I have aimed to implement the challenge and stopped a few times per day, or if I am approaching a difficult situation I find checking in with myself provides me with the ability to make changes before the event comes. This morning, I started initial consultations on two friends who I am training at the gym. I was so nervous, but checked in. And as I was getting prepared, my colleague and supervisor said to me, "OWN IT". So I decided I would! The consultations were great. My plan worked. So really, I didn't need to worry for the previous day and half!"

Chantal Staaf said, "This is probably the hardest one for me so far. I am SUPER good at not having great feelings about myself. Despite the fact I KNOW how toxic it is AND how much it makes a huge difference in our everyday life. I usually fill other people's cups with good vibes, but never take the time to do it for myself. So the hourly challenge will be super for me to take part in. It will be a challenge for sure, but one I am ready and willing to embrace it."

Sandra Girard shared in the Dynamic You™ Community, "I like the hourly reminder idea. I am checking in with myself and focusing on doing less things well, "unscheduling" myself. I like to be involved and busy, but everything tends to come at once. I am pushing the reset button more."

CHAPTER 7
PILLAR 6: BE MAGNETIC

We're more than halfway through, woohoo! I want to take a moment and ask how you're doing. Have you been committing fully to the process? Are you still making lots of time to implement the Pillars and then commenting on the Dynamic You™ Global Community Page? If you haven't been doing either of these steps, or you feel you want to take it up a level, great. Now is the time to recommit.

What does recommitting look like? When you recommit you actually sit and say, "I am going to fully commit to this process. I'm going to jump back in. Or I'm going to be consistent in what I'm doing because I'm already doing a great job." Whatever it is, recommit, fully commit, commit more. Whatever that looks like for you. This is sometimes what Dynamic Women™ have to do. We have all the best intentions. We have every considerable motivation, and then we somehow fall off, life gets in the way or old habits resurface. This is my invitation for you to recommit. You are worth it!

Grab your phone, grab your calendar, and make a date with yourself to do the different steps. That could mean you set a schedule to read each Pillar, set times where you'll do the challenges. And then, over the course of the next few days, interact with the other ladies on the Global Community group. I know women love being connected with others, especially when they're learning and receiving support. Your experience will be much richer if you choose to connect with the other Dynamic Women™ in this community.

I want you to get the most out of this book, just like the ladies in the program. I didn't design it to just be shelf help or merely another file or another item on your To-Do list. I want you to thoroughly do this because I've seen what happens when women step into these nine Pillars and practice them wholeheartedly. They unleash the Dynamic Woman™ in themselves.

We're going to be jumping into the next Pillar. So if you want to take a moment to recommit and spend some time with your scheduler to figure out when you're going to do certain things, take that time now.

What Is The Sixth Pillar?

Be magnetic. What do I mean by being magnetic? I've frequently referred to that sensation of being in a room and seeing someone special.

That someone is surrounded by people, and when you first see her, you think, "I need to talk to that person." Dynamic Women™ keep a little bit of magic up their sleeves, and it draws other people to them. It draws friendships, maybe it draws men, and it draws opportunities, business, and clients. Whatever you want. You feel like this person is a living magnet, attracting all these people and things to them. Does this sound like something you want to have or have more of? Yes! For sure!

Let me break this down. Being magnetic is actually a state of being. It's less about doing and more about being. In the first few Pillars, we talked about things you can do, like being prioritized. This is a way of being, being prioritized. However, there are things you have to do in order to be prioritized, where being magnetic is how you're acting.

If you recall, a lot of people were really keen on the Law of Attraction and its ideas, presented in the book and movie called <u>The Secret</u>. Basically, the Law of Attraction says that whatever you put out there is exactly what you're going to receive in return. The secret is to attract the things you want to yourself. We want to be thinking about that, that a magnet is attracting and pulling in what it's putting out.

Think about emanating good vibes, good magnetic vibes. If you've ever held magnets in your hand, you've felt the power between them as they are drawn together or when they repel each other. That is the invisible force we want to create in ourselves. That same force can be used with people, and you can tap into that power by just being and knowing that what you put out, you get back.

What Is Being Magnetic Made Of?

Some people feel that magnetic people are that way because they are charismatic. That is one way to be magnetic and I could have called this Pillar charisma. But what I find, especially in women, is that they already feel pressured to be charismatic, and the word itself weighs on them heavily. It makes us feel like either we have it or we don't. Some people are certainly and undeniably born with it, and often that leaves the rest of us feeling like we're somehow hopeless and less for it. We tell ourselves, "I'm not very charismatic, never have been." I don't want you to feel that way. Because being magnetic is something that is attainable, you can work at it.

I want to spend a moment speaking about charisma because I think this is important. Now, charisma comes from your presence, your power, and your warmth. I'll explain each one separately.

Presence

Your presence has to do with how present you are in the moment, how present you are with other people. Your presence is how you hold yourself, and how people can get an idea of you and what you're about just by being around you. To be present and have your presence felt more strongly is pretty simple. It just requires you to be more mindful, more mentally, emotionally, and spiritually present in your interactions with people. You don't have to be way out there with brilliant ideas and exceptional observations, you just need to be grounded in the moment.

Power

The next is power, and there is a lot to know about power. It can be seen as a negative thing because there are people out there who abuse their power. Actually, I created a program called Dynamic Power™ where I delve deeper into the art of having and using power. I don't want to elaborate too much because there are so many nuances to power and pre-misconceptions about what power is. Briefly, power allows you to positively influence a situation, inspire people, get things happening and increase your results.

You Can Be in or Out of Power in Three Ways

1. **Power Over** where you use your power in a negative way to dominate, walk all over and intimidate others, so ultimately you take their power.

2. **Power Under** where you don't have a voice or an opinion and get taken advantage of because you lose your power, give it away, or others take your power away from you.

3. Ideally you want to be somewhere in the middle when you are in your **Personal Power Sweet Spot™**. Where you have power and use it in your favor, but you create the power rather than striping it away from anyone. That's what I teach. When you can step into your Personal Power Sweet Spot™, you'll possess a stronger presence and have more confidence. You'll be able to start making things happen around you. Again, it comes back to being magnetic. Since I teach Dynamic Power™ over a six-month program, that's why magnetic is the Pillar. Everyone can relate a little bit easier to it.

Warmth

The last attribute of being magnetic is warmth. Being warm is being approachable, making others feel welcome, and putting in effort to connect. When it comes to being magnetic, I'm going to really emphasize this one because so many people tell themselves, "I'm not outgoing. I'm not going to be the life of the party. I'm can't do all that stuff to pull people in." That's okay. You can practice being warm if that feels like the best way for you to be magnetic. I'm going to explain a little bit more about how that works.

Three Ways To Be Magnetic

Read over the three ways to be magnetic and see which ones you feel you already use and which ones you want to bring in. Or maybe you're using a little bit of each one and you want to use more of them all. You decide what is best for you. I'll go through each one.

1. Be Passion and Purpose Driven

You know when you're listening to someone speak about her passion and her purpose, there is just this attraction because she is so excited.

For example, if I was to tell you about my day and I said, "I did the dishes. There were so many of them and so I had them all over the stove and filling up my sink, but I got them done." Or, "I got some help with my taxes," these are not very exciting things. Even if you talk about your job, unless you love it, talking about it emits a low energy frequency.

But when you talk about your passion and your purpose, you sound like this. "Oh my gosh. I'm writing this book because I know women are more dynamic than they show. It all started with my love for the Dynamic Women™ in Action community because I get to bring these women together, teach them, provide Coaching in Action™ and see the friendships that form and how they're collaborating with each other. It's so important that we network on a deeper level rather than that service level where everyone's just slinging cards around. It fills me up to hear the success stories and the impact that it all has on these amazing women. I want to do this forever!" I could keep going, but you get the idea. You know how you feel when you're talking about your passion or your purposes. It's the difference between talking about your favorite person, whether it's a celebrity or a musician, and talking about someone who's wronged you recently. Could you feel your energy go up and then down even just reading those words?

When you're talking about your passion, you feel motivated and others around you feel the same. It's great if you're trying to get a client or a customer. It also attracts others to you because when you're speaking this way or you're acting this way, people love it. There's an underlying energy there that they're drawn to. That's the magnetic part. Be passionate and purpose driven. If you don't know what you're passion is, figure it out.

For whatever reason, if your current passion doesn't feel or sound exciting, find out the underlying why. The why of what you do what you do. There's always a reason. You can find out by asking yourself, "Why do I do what I do?" You might say, "Oh, I want to help people." Well, doesn't almost everybody? Why do you want to help people? What do they get out of it? Then ask yourself, what's important about that? Then ask yourself what's important about that? Every answer you give, keep asking yourself what's important and why it's important, and keep asking yourself until you get to the underlying reason. Being purpose and passion driven is the first part of being magnetic.

2. Be Positive.

Yes, we can truly be positive, and being positive starts with our beliefs. How do you make your beliefs positive? Well, you begin with gratitude. Gratitude for what's important to you, for what you have, for what's possible, and just giving thanks for everything. That's a really great way to start the positivity.

Some people think, "Well, I'm not always positive." Sometimes negative things happen. That's okay. But it doesn't mean you walk around being negative about everything all the time. You can build a strong foundation in being positive by starting with your beliefs. Why? Well, when you have positive beliefs, they become your thoughts, those thoughts become your words, and those words become your actions, and ultimately, your reactions to negative things.

Positivity is vital if you want to be magnetic. We all know what it feels like to talk to an optimistic person. I'm not saying be positive all the time, because we want to be real, like Pillar Two. But we do want to be positive as much as possible because it raises our energy. And when we're talking to somebody else, it raises her energy too. Think about what it's like to talk to someone who is negative about everything. She complains about her kids and her husband. She complains about the weather. She complains about her business and finances. She views everything pessimistically, never attempting to look at the bright side of things. When you talk to a pessimist for too long, it becomes physically exhausting. It's one thing to process an unfortunate event and talk about it with a loved one, but it's another to just complain and whine every chance you get. We need to take ownership of our perspectives, and being grateful and positive is one way of doing that.

There's a Cherokee Indian Legend called Two Wolves, which is a parable of a grandfather telling his grandson about the inner battle that takes place inside us between our positive and negative thoughts. Here is how the story goes:

> An old Cherokee is teaching his grandson about life. "A fight is going on inside me," he said to the boy.
>
> "It is a terrible fight and it is between two wolves. One is evil – he is anger, envy, sorrow, regret, greed, arrogance, self-pity, guilt, resentment, inferiority, lies, false pride, superiority, and ego."
>
> He continued, "The other is good – he is joy, peace, love, hope, serenity, humility, kindness, benevolence, empathy, generosity, truth, compassion, and faith. The same fight is going on inside you – and inside every other person, too."
>
> The grandson thought about it for a minute and then asked his grandfather, "Which wolf will win?"
>
> The old Cherokee simply replied, "The one you feed."

You can think about this as Dynamic You™ versus your saboteur. Which wolf, which part of you do you choose to feed? Do you feed the positive side or the negative? The side that is the Dynamic You™ or your saboteur?

Again, it all starts with your beliefs. Your beliefs create your thoughts, which create your words, and then create your actions. The great thing is if you're interacting with somebody who's positive, what's going to happen? There's going to be a positive reaction from your action, right? We always want to be around positive people who lift us up and help us out.

When you are thinking of others who are magnetic, just think of the level of positivity they exude. Check in with yourself and ask yourself:

- How much positivity do I exude?
- Where am I when I'm more positive?
- When are you feeling a bit negative or down?

Tazeem Jamal shared about having a high level of positivity. "Sometimes I feel like my level of being magnetic is different than others. Sometimes my high energy can intimidate others or make them feel like I have too much. How do I navigate through certain situations and how do I scale back? I don't want to sound aggressive or pushy and then also not too low key." I asked everyone in the program how they felt about *Tazeem's* energy and they all said they thought she was great and shouldn't worry anymore. And think if we hadn't brought this up, *Tazeem* would still be concerned with how she was and might turn down how magnetic she is.

Being magnetic is less about having high energy than it is about being too opinionated, not listening, or being in a **power over** position. The key is to make sure we give others time and space to share, especially when in a group or team setting. You can always check in with yourself and read the other person's cues:

- Is she withdrawing?
- Does she seem distracted?
- Is she only nodding her head?
- Is she looking at a clock or phone like she needs to go?

If you feel like you haven't been magnetic, the best and quickest way to re-engage someone is to ask an open ended question, something that can't be answered with a one word yes or no.

For example, I had a friend who was at a time in her life where she was frequently more negative than positive. We'd hang out and when we'd finish, she'd say, "Oh my gosh. Thanks for listening to me. I feel so much better," because she'd basically whined and complained the whole time. But relieving those feelings from her just felt as though she dumped them on me. I'd walk out of there feeling tired and worn out, like I had no energy and it was me who was in a terrible mood by the end. I knew if our friendship was going to continue, something had to change.

When people are too negative, we don't want to be around them, even if we care for them deeply. When she'd ask me to do something, I'd ask myself, "Do I have enough energy for this?" When we hang out with our friends, this isn't a question we should be asking yourselves. Being with friends should add to our energy source, not bankrupt it. We want to be uppers, not downers in people's lives. We want to fill people's cups, not deplete them. If you want to be a magnetic person, think about how you can be more positive.

I was in a business situation at a networking dinner and there were people flanking both sides of me. I was having a wonderful conversation with one lady, but when I turned to engage with the person on the other side of me, she immediately started complaining about stuff. I felt like I was trapped.

I was interested in her business and curious about what she did, but her negativity and complaining had me imagining future engagements with her. I thought, " If I'm working with her, is her negativity going to come into our business relationship?" In the end, I didn't make any plans for a follow up because I'm protective of my energy. You should be protective of your energy as well. For you to go out into the world and be magnetic and be positive, maybe you need to be a little bit protective of who's around you. We go back to the Pillar Connection and our five power people around us at our board. Since we're the average of the people we spend the most time with, we have to pick and choose who will impact and influence us in the right way. And if you want people to spend time with you, being positive is an important factor in that.

3. Be Approachable.

It's the warmth in your charisma. When you're approachable, you're present. You are there. You have a kindness about you. You focus on who the person is, rather than what she does. Being approachable is being inclusive. Again, we're getting rid of all judgment. You're adapting to situations, not judging them. You act approachable by having an open body stance and posture. Don't cross your arms or wear a stern facial expression. Be present and conscious, have an approachable calmness about you.

It can be as simple as just standing with an open stance and wearing the warmth of a smile. Those are really simple things. When you're chatting with people and others come to join in, be the one to open up the circle and welcome them into the conversation. Be curious about them. Invite them to share things about themselves, things that are important to them.

So often, we're in our own heads trying to figure out what we're going to say next. I'm not saying anything new here, you know that. You've been in situations where you see the other person is physically there but not mentally present. That what you're saying just seems to be going right over her head, in one ear and out the other. There's nothing worse than talking to somebody and knowing that she doesn't really care what you're saying and she's not really listening anyway.

So often, people don't listen to us. Sometimes it comes from her insecurities because she's figuring out what she needs to say next and worried about saying the right thing or coming across the wrong way. It's best to just look at the person and listen.

With social media and all the time spent putting stuff out there, we don't really know if people are listening. So in person, there's nothing better than telling someone something that's important to you and having her listen. It makes you feel good. If you can be the person that provides that for someone else, she is going to be so grateful and she is going to want to hang out with you more.

Magnetic people are approachable. If you make others feel important by listening to them, by being curious and reacting to what they share in a favorable way, you are going to continue to be magnetic. You're going to motivate people out there to talk about you in such a positive way.

Which ones are you? *Melody Owen* reflected and shared, "I think that I am a warm person, approachable and wanting to connect with others. I am open, curious and nonjudgmental."

Having a nice blend of all of these things is important, which will pull up your confidence, your presence and your power, the other aspects of charisma. For example, if you only have warmth and you're always listening, there's never going to be a time where you shine and people are going to walk all over you. So make sure you blend of all of these nicely.

Here is Your Challenge

I've got a challenge for you. Are you ready? I hope so. What you're going to do is grab an elastic and put it around your wrist. For 24 hours you're going to focus on the positivity aspect of being magnetic. The elastic is your reminder, and anytime in the next 24 hours, you think a negative thought, a negative word, a negative action, you're going flick it. Yes, it hurts a little bit, but you'll be okay. Just anytime you have a negative thought, pull that rubber band.

We're going to use it to evaluate when we are feeding the wrong wolf, the saboteur. We're retraining ourselves to be believing, thinking, speaking, and acting more positively. For the next 24 hours, will you do it? Yes? I hope so. When you begin this challenge, please go on the Community Page and write, "I'm starting my 24-hour challenge," and add whatever else you want to say. Let us know you're starting. Then give us updates as to how it's going. Share how many times you've had to flick it. I really hope you don't do it so much or so hard that you break your elastic. It's happened before. If you don't own any elastics, go buy some.

The second part of the challenge is to work on being more approachable and upping your passion and purpose. When you're talking with someone, I would love for you to find out something about them, by being curious and listening and pulling stuff out, find something lovely about them and acknowledge them for it or compliment them for it. I'm going to share how you do that. For my clients, and the ladies who've been at Dynamic Women™ in Action events, you know how this goes. To acknowledge the other person, you're going to do it with four or five words.

How to Acknowledge

This is the way the FIVE word Acknowledgment goes.

- You are an <u>adjective</u> <u>title</u>.
- You are a <u>smart</u> <u>businesswoman</u>.

I'll give you a few examples.

- You are a loving mother.
- You are a creative designer.
- You are a fantastic wife (friend, employee).

You are an <u>adjective</u> and then her <u>title</u>. Don't say anything else. Don't say because you did this for me. Because I'll tell you, the person is going to go straight to what you said at the end and evaluate that, judge that. Those five words are the simplest, most powerful gift you could give someone else. It's a word gift, a compliment.

The FIVE word Acknowledgment is one way. Here's how to use it in four words.

- You're an <u>adjective</u> <u>title</u>.
- You're a <u>loyal</u> <u>friend</u>.

Super simple. I'm not getting all crazy and complicated on you here. But I'll tell you, if you're in that moment of being approachable, being present, really connecting and listening to a person and then you say, "Wow, you're such a loving mother," or "You're an incredible friend," or "You're a passionate business owner." Whatever you want to say, if you deliver it in that way, oh my gosh, her heart is going to melt. You've just given her the greatest gift and you've become magnetic because she is going to want more of that.

You're doing it in such an authentic way that it builds positivity and awesomeness and love in the world. It's going to ripple out. When you give that word gift, this acknowledgment to another person, she is then going to turn around and it's going to positively affect her whole day. Imagine if you received an acknowledgment like this, you'd definitely feel positive and confident, and you'd feel motivated to try even harder. Let us know how it goes. Whom did you compliment and how did she receive it? How did you feel for giving her that? The amazing thing is giving these word gifts is free.

I challenge you to connect with more people, get to know them better and give acknowledgments. Of course, don't forget to do your 24-hour elastic challenge, practice making your beliefs, your thoughts, your words and your actions positive.

How Was The Challenge?

Sandra Girard, "What makes me magnetic is I am positive, approachable and interested in learning more about others. I share my stories and experiences with others."

Chantal Staaf, "The elastic Band is a terrific visual of how negative we think/speak and act. What makes me magnetic is all 3 to be honest; with the 'bigger one being positive (which I haven't totally been in quite a while now). I have awesome energy and people LOVE being around me. Which is why I LOVE my business and perhaps how I've been in a negative space lately. I LOVED LOVED LOVED 'feeding the positive' wolf. I am the type of person who sees the glass full instead of half empty. I do make a huge effort to acknowledge beautiful things about people. I agree people are so quick to share when they are yucky or things are not working, but I have found that giving someone that pat on the back truly makes their day or turns it around."

Cora Naylor, "I really enjoy meeting and getting to know people. Over the last few years I have really worked on asking questions to get others talking about themselves. I used to be a lot more introverted, but because of my business I needed to come out of myself more. I truly love finding out what other people do and why—so I find it easier to ask the questions and let others do most of the talking (most people like talking about themselves). I am working on feeling more "magnetic" when I am in groups where I don't know people, [and] in those instances, I tend to draw back into myself. Some days are better than others, depending how 'on' I'm feeling.

Claudine Pender, Magnetic!! I'm magnetic because I am positive, KIND and very enthusiastic about what other people do. I love to help and do my best to contribute in my community. I wear the biggest smile and always want to make people feel welcome. Even though I love to talk, I LISTEN and I am open to learning and growing. I am funny AND I can laugh at myself, too!"

Elaine asked, "How do you stop being magnetic to needy people? Do you turn off the magnet?"

Consider being magnetic on different levels. You need to create your own levels of intimacy, connection, and decide when and who gets the most of you. For example, if I had to make some generic levels, here's how I'd design them:

1. Your family is closest to you: your spouse, kids and parents. This could even include your siblings, aunts and uncles, and grandparents. They get hugs, words of love and connection, kind deeds, information, your time and they are a priority.

2. Then would be your closest friends. They get a lot of the same things as above.

3. Next would be your favorite colleagues, clients, and people in other areas of life, such as your coach, trainer, mentor, etc. They get your time, gratitude and honesty.

4. This could be people you really like, aren't very close to, but would like to be. You are pretty open with them and show your loving side, but not to the level of the groups before them.

5. These are acquaintances, so parents of your kids' friends, the sports coaches and teachers, your suppliers, people who are in your networking circle you don't know very well. You probably don't hug them. You are real with them, but not transparent and overly kind. You don't go out of your way for this set of people.

6. People you meet for the first time. Similar to the group before, but since this is your first time meeting them, your focus is on getting to know them and seeing what connection you do have before you are too magnetic.

Writing this out feels a little strange for me because a strong value of mine is being inclusive: making sure everyone feels included and belongs. Over the years, I have realized, yes, you need people to feel welcome and comfortable, but when I try to connect with them on the same level I do with my level two ladies, there is an unbalance.

Those closer to me notice, and it messes with my levels of priority. Also, they haven't earned a Level Two connection yet, so it's a little too much too soon. It's like going through all of the bases on a first date. Too much too soon.

Additionally, I used to be under the impression that everyone has good intentions, but this isn't always the case. I have been burned before by people who were like a wolf in sheep's clothing. Since I brought them in too quickly, I didn't get a chance to get to know them, their true intentions, or even use my intuition to feel them out. They then asked me for things like money and high-level introductions. They asked to collaborate and used ideas I shared with them as their own. I'm not saying people are bad. I'm only saying you have to look out for yourself and save your energy, your time, and your gifts for those already on your priority list.

What I'd love for you to share is tell us what makes you magnetic. What part of those three is easier for you? Passion or purpose, positive or approachable? Which of those three do you think is the one that you can do really well and share that with us?

How Was The 24 Hour Elastic Band Challenge?

Pam Karlen shared, "I am pretty much a positive person, but just having the elastic band on my wrist was a good reminder that if I was starting to go there I could stop myself to stay positive. I was at a play and the sound was really bad and I could have just beat the play up because of that because we couldn't hear. Instead I knew that I wasn't going to go there and instead enjoy the play for what it was."

Cora Naylor, "I had a good day and it was a busy day, but I saw the band on my wrist all day. So I wonder if I had a positive day just because I saw the band there."

Tazeem Jamal, "I have actually done this challenge many time before, but not for a long time so when you challenged us to it I thought how cool. It has been a really full few weeks for me and so wearing it helped me to shift my perspective from a negative before I actually went there. I think it's something we should bring back every month!"

CHAPTER 8
PILLAR 7: COLLABORATE

Now we're ready to talk about Pillar number seven. Pillar seven is collaboration. Are you collaborating already, maybe in your life, or in your business? Are you wondering, "Oh, I don't know if I am." Well, I'm going to show you the many, many ways you are probably already collaborating.

What is Collaborating?

Collaboration is the act of working with someone to produce or create something new. When we were children, we were told many times to cooperate, to play nicely, and that sharing is caring! For me, cooperation stood out as being very important. Collaboration is similar to cooperation, but when you collaborate, you are working closely together in a more intimate way, probably for a longer time period, and with a bigger goal in mind.

Collaboration leaves you with a sense of abundance. Both collaboration and cooperation are the opposite of competition. Competition is terrible because when we compete, the feeling of scarcity emerges. We lack confidence, feel threatened along with all the negativity that accompanies it. But we don't want negativity, do we? Collaboration helps us remain positive and work together. When you work together like that, you're a team. It feels good to be part of a team because other people support you.

When you look at a partnership, a pair of people working like a team, it's two people collaborating. But when you add up the results, it actually equals three because there's something dynamic about working alongside someone else. It elevates your own qualities. If you're lucky, each of you gets to focus on what you're naturally skilled at, covering what the other person isn't as good at, so you're only getting the best of both of you. When you put that together, it gives you even better results. Each one can stand in her own power and her own strengths, and when you put them together, the result is multiplied once more. There's power in one, but there's more power in many. There's also excitement and energy. You can feed off each other, off that support, off that idea, off that passion, off whatever the other person is feeling, you can feed off it. Hopefully, both of you are using the previous Pillars, such as, Magnetic, Real, Connected, etc. because otherwise, the partnership is not going to go very well.

There are many ways and styles in which to collaborate. During my research, it totally blew my mind as to how many ways I could collaborate, rather than the obvious, "I'm going to work with another business owner to put on an event." Collaboration is bigger than that. I have listed 16 different styles that I'm going to take you through. I'm going to give you examples of how they fit into business and then how they fit into life. You can start to see what they do and what you could do. That's your intention in reading these: consider where you have already performed these styles in business, and where you have done this or that in life. Think about other opportunities to collaborate in business and life in the future. Write down in your journal the ones you've done or any ideas you come up with.

16 Ways to Collaborate

	The Way to Collaborate with a Professional Example	The Way to Collaborate with a Personal Example
1	**Creation Of A Document:** Maybe you've used Google Docs or Google Sheets before, and you've worked closely with somebody at work or someone at your business to create some sort of document. It might even be with a lawyer, you with your financial adviser or a tax person, bookkeeper, whatever. You're working together to make that document finalized.	In life, maybe you use a family calendar and it's on the wall and you write stuff on it and your partner writes stuff on it too. Maybe your kids contribute to its contents as well, maybe your own parents do too. Or maybe it's on your phone and it's connected to everyone else who needs access to it.
2	**Event Collaboration:** In business, it's great to collaborate on events. You've seen it happen many times, I'm sure, because the great thing is you share the costs, you share the marketing, and you are then both sending it out to your lists. If you're both speaking at it, you're sharing the responsibility	In my own life, this happens every year in December. Another mom and I collaborate on the birthday parties of our kids because they're not too far apart and we have a very close circle of friends. Rather than ask people to go to two separate parties, on two different weekends, or ask them attend two parties on the same day, or even worse at the exact same

	of education and value. There are lots of ways you get to share the responsibility.	time, we decided to put it together because all the same people are attending. With our combined parties, we only need to provide one set of cupcakes or one big cake, one spread of food, and only one activity. It's so much easier.
3	**Educational Information:** Maybe you plan a webinar or an interview or something similar is going to happen. Whoever's collaborating can share it with her list. There are a few different ways. Maybe I interview someone, and we're collaborating together for my podcast or my webinar, whatever I'm using it for. But then she gets the benefit of that as well. There are many styles of two people working together, as well as a telesummit with many people working together with the person who put it on.	For the personalized one, it might be sharing information in a neighborhood watch or a block watch or something where everybody gets an email regarding what's happening and then shares it with her people.
4	**A Trade Or A Barter:** I'm sure you've heard a lot bartering in business. I don't need to give you many examples. It's pretty simple. For example, one person gives printing services and the other does her website. Or photography for a membership in a group etc.	But you might be wondering, "How do I barter or trade with people in my personal life?" It could be something like trading money for your kids doing different chores around the house. It could also be sharing the responsibility of getting kids to and from school. You might trade jam for snow shovelling or dog walking for mail pick up when you're on holiday. That's collaborating with a trade or barter.

5	**Getting A Job Done Or Working On A Project Together:** Have you been at a job or somewhere where you've put a team together, like with volunteering, where you're together on a project to put on an event or to work with a specific client. That's getting a job done.	With your personal life, it might simply be cleaning your house. It needs to get done and everybody pitches in. You're collaborating.
6	**Clinics:** You have probably been to a clinic where they have an acupuncturist, a massage therapist, a chiropractor and a naturopath. All of these different types of health professionals are working together for the common goal of having a thriving clinic.	In your personal life, you may think of it like your strata. Everybody's working together in order to achieve that common goal of living in a wonderful community or wonderful neighborhood.
7	**Co-Working Spaces:** Obviously, not all the people that work at co-working spaces are collaborating in their profession, but they are talking to each other, maybe even supporting each other, and creating a good workplace atmosphere. Everyone is pitching in, and by paying to be there, everyone gets to belong to a co-working unit, each person has an office.	In your personal life, it might be something like people in a band. To make good music, to make things work, everybody has to play her instrument in a certain way and work together and harmonize.

| 8 | **With A Client:**

For example, getting a project launched, helping someone finish her book, or get her product marketing sold. While you don't necessarily reap the benefits of the product or book sales, you're collaborating and you're working together to help that thing happen. This also happens with service-based businesses. With my clients, I am collaborating with them to accomplish whatever they want from their business and from their lives. | A personal example would be kids' homework. Their homework is their goal, just like with a business client relationship. You're supporting them and collaborating with them to help them get it done. |
|---|---|---|
| 9 | **With a Charity:**

You've probably seen in real life, you go to the supermarket, or somewhere else and the cashier asks, "Would you like to donate a dollar to whatever?" That's a way that a business has collaborated with a charity. Other ways are silent auctions, where the event has one purpose but they've collaborated and joined with a charity to use the great opportunity of having a room full of people who also believe in that cause. | An example of this in personal life would be a school fundraiser. The fundraising company collaborates with the school to bring the money in, then the kids all work together to raise money for the school. |
| 10 | **To Recycle And Reuse Industrial Waste:**

You've probably heard many times where one company goes to throw something away, some | At home, we recycle. We just take our waste and hand it off to the recycling depot, or it gets picked up with our garbage and taken to companies who can reuse it. That's our way of collaborating |

	sort of by-product, and another company scoops it up and reuses it. One example is in making chocolate. The by-product is the cocoa shells; these shells can be used in mulch for plants (which I bought for my Dad) or even for tea (which I drink). Another example is Color By Amber. Some of their interlays are the end cuts of Tibetan prayer flags. They take the scrap cuts of that flag that would have been thrown away. They pay for the scraps and use it in their jewellery, which is also made from recycled plastic.	with the recycling companies to make that happen.
11	**Deals and Coupons:** This happened recently when I was at a play center with my kids. When I paid for their tickets, I was handed two coupons for a free kid's meal with the purchase of an adult meal. That's where you've got two businesses working together to give a deal.	Now, for this in personal life, it's a little bit harder to know how you would get a deal. It's similar to the point we made when we discussed bartering and trading. It might be something as simple as asking your husband to do the dishes and you'll vacuum. Or saying, "I'll take the dog out in the morning if I can take the car to work."
12	**Providing Your Clients With A New Product:** For example, I was having lunch with the CFO of a major Yoga studio. She was explaining that they carry supplements in their studios for their clients. They do not carry their own product, but their clients like that brand. I'm sure you've been	In our personal lives, we do this without even recognizing it. Sharing recipes, making product recommendations to friends and family. Or say your friend has a problem and you know someone who's better suited than you are to provide advice on that particular issue. So you bring two people together. Anytime you make a

	to many places where they offer someone else's product because they thought you might enjoy it.	referral in your personal life, it's as if you're selling someone else's product.
13	**Piggybacking Off Another Company:** An example with Burger King® will illustrate the concept well. I read about how Burger King wanted to easily get into Spain. What they did was collaborate with a gas station chain, to get exclusive rights to put their Burger King® restaurants inside the gas stations. That allowed Burger King® to piggyback off the success of the gas station. The gas station already had customers, and so Burger King® piggybacked access to those established customers. Burger King® was able to break into the market really quickly with the support of a trusted brand. You've probably seen that happen often.	In personal life, this can happen when you're new somewhere and you find the person who knows everybody and you ask them to introduce you to people. Again, you're piggybacking off of the success that they've already had. You're doing it in a way that's mutually beneficial, because if they introduced a cool person to their friends, it's a win-win all over.
14	**Using A Product To Provide A Service:** For example, one of my Dynamic Women™ in Action members is a Certified facilitator of Lego® Serious Play® workshops. She uses Lego to teach leadership and do personal development training rather than just as a kid's toy.	

15	**A Product Is Repackaged:** For example, one of my clients, who makes dog treats, was approached by someone who wanted to create a dog treat that had hemp in it. She's agreed to do the baking and he's going to repackage the product. I also met someone who owns a soup company, and what she does is buys the soup from a catering company and then packages it, brands it and then she sells it. Buying their product and then putting it out there as your own is collaboration.	
16	**Groups:** The last one is in all groups where collaboration is apparent; businesses, coaching circles, masterminds, accountability groups, etc. The list goes on as to all the places you can find collaboration.	Families, neighborhoods, teams, volunteering, clubs, churches etc.

How many of those have you been part of? Share with the Global Community! Look at the 16 plus ways you can collaborate, and let us know one of those that you've already done. Tell us how it went, how you enjoyed it. Was it a good collaboration process? Or would you make changes next time?

Do you see an opportunity where you could do some collaborating? Well, before you do, let me give you the seven secrets to a great collaboration. You need to know these.

Seven Secrets To Having A Great Collaboration

1. **First, choose your participants wisely.** If you're going to cooperate with her, you want to know she is a good person. You want to know that you hold the same values. You want to know your vision for where you're going is the same. Then, when you read the other six, know if this person will be able to follow along with them.

2. **Second, you'll need to be honest.** If you have a certain expectation, say it upfront. I spend a lot of my time designing relationships, especially between business owners or people collaborating on a project. Anytime I collaborate with someone else on a project, I spend quite a bit of time designing how we're going to work together, what that looks like, even the exit strategy, or if it fails, what we're going to do. If something is not going right during this process, speak up. Otherwise, the collaboration will be terrible and the result will not be what you intended. You don't want it to be a waste of time.

3. **Three, create communication guidelines.** Is there a specific way you want to communicate? It could be a one-hour long phone call every Monday morning, with an agenda of items you need to discuss. Develop a plan for how to communicate if something upsets either one of you. If you don't set guidelines for how you're going to communicate, you might find that your business partner is texting you at all hours or calling you every five minutes when small things come up. Choose how you're going to communicate with each other.

4. **Four, have everyone equally participate.** That's on a few different fronts. If you're having a brainstorming session, make sure everyone gets to speak. If you're all collaborating, every voice needs to be heard. You never know what someone else has to say and what her idea might be. It could completely shift how you do things. By not giving everyone time to be heard, confusion could arise as well. If everyone doesn't get her moment to speak and ask questions, you might find that there's some animosity or that some ideas or points are missed. That's only one part of participating. The other part is making sure everybody has an equal role, or at least it's known who doesn't have a role, if that's the way it is. Sometimes, there are people who do the work and there are people who put in the money. That's how you collaborate. Any way is okay but it needs to be clear.

5. That leads to the next point. **Number five is to make sure you design the roles and assign accountability.** Make sure everybody knows her job description and what her part of the collaboration is, what she is responsible for, what happens if she doesn't do it. Then hold each other accountable. For example, you have this task to do and you need to do it by

Friday at this time every week. You need to make sure that you have something in place where if the task doesn't happen, you know what the next steps are to take. It's not like there's one boss who is overseeing you collaborating on a project. Everyone oversees each other.

6. **Next, outline a clear goal and timeline.** If you don't know the destination, it's really hard to reach it. If you do reach your destination, it may be through a path that isn't as efficient as others, wasting time and money. Without a timeline, your own work that is separate from the project's work could take precedence or the personal work of the person you are collaborating with could become a priority over the collaboration. Make sure you write out clear goals and timelines and everyone in the collaboration approves.

7. **Last, recognize accomplishment.** If the person you're working with is doing an awesome job, let them know. Use an acknowledgment like what I shared earlier. Set something up so that if the other person isn't good at recognizing you, there's something in place so you do get recognized.

Designing Relationships

Designing relationships is important for collaborations, and even for friendships and any other relationships. The other person has to be a willing partner in designing things. Whether in a partnership or a group, each person needs to decide the following and a discussion between all parties needs to happen:

- Each person's intention for the collaboration
- Each person's vision for the relationship and the project
- Each person's roles and responsibilities
- A timeline for the project and those roles
- Each person's values
- What are the expectations of each person and why that's important to them
- An exit strategy for business relationships

I always design relationships with my clients and they share what they expect from me and the assumptions they made. I share with them what I am committing and what I expect from them as clients, such as to show up on time and to send me their Preparation Form in advance. We establish everything in before we work together so no one is uncomfortable later on. Then if someone feels like an aspect of our working relationship isn't working, they don't struggle to communicate it, and have tools to communicate it rather than speaking bluntly which can result in the other party feeling hurt and becoming defensive.

By asking questions about future situations, you can also decide how things will be in the present. For example, if someone doesn't meet a deadline, how do we respond? When someone wants to bring someone else into the collaboration, how do we measure if she is a good fit?

Instead, you have the opportunity to Redesign the Relationship. It takes the emotion out of it. You're not attacking the person because the relationship has been given the power. You're redesigning the relationship not the people in it.

Michelle Abraham said that she has never had an issue being honest with someone when collaborating thanks to designing relationships. She has found each person needs to be clear of her own vision and be honest with how much time and what work hours she can give to the group setting.

It's Never Too Late To Redesign A Relationship

If you're asking, What if the relationship was never designed? What if it's failing? Good news! You can still design or redesign it! Start by asking yourself these questions when looking at all of your current relationships:

- Do I like how this relationship is?
- If you don't like it: What is missing and what do I want to change?
- If you do like it: How can I improve this already solid relationship and/or collaboration?

For professional relationships, create a formal atmosphere for that conversation. Go for lunch, call a meeting, meet for coffee. Whatever you choose, face-to-face is best so you can read the other person's non-verbal cues. Let her know in advance what you want to meet for so she can be prepared. Here are some ways to do that:

- "Hey I want to talk about where we are going in the next six months. When are you free?"
- "I'd like to talk about how we work together, can we do that?"

Then you can ask specific questions in advance so she has time to think.

- What do you need to get from this relationship so your needs are met?
- What do you need more of from me?
- What do you want to do more of yourself?
- What could I do that would make you angry, annoyed or frustrated? (This is a really good question when designing things from the beginning because you haven't had a chance to do this at all. If you're redesigning, then you have a chance of them saying something that you have done.)

If you have designed the relationship once, then you can set the date for when you will revisit the relationship. Say, three months later, at the end of the project, quarterly or yearly. And if you need to redesign earlier, you can easily say, "Hey can we redesign the relationship this week?"

These conversations allow you to say things that might feel uncomfortable, things you've wanted to say for a while. If it still seems difficult, or if you are part of a group, then bring a trained coach in to do this. I'm often hired to facilitate the designing or redesigning of groups when everyone is an equal partner. That way, everyone is heard and I can translate and reframe what people really want so everyone gets her needs met and/or compromises are made.

Maria Peebles used these tools and techniques in her life right when she learned about this Pillar. "Starting my career I had a mentor, then I became her assistant and both of those relationships seemed to have clear roles. But recently, I stepped into my full role and became her colleague, so things now are not going as well as before. After this Pillar, I knew we had to redesign the relationship because where I am now, and where I was before are so different. Thanks to this Pillar, I had great words and tools to help me have that conversation and redesign the relationship. It helped [me] to…realize what the challenges were, then to be able to put words to them and specifically what was missing and what we would need [in order] to be able to redesign things."

Here is Your Challenge

Do you have all your info now? Do you know how to make a great collaboration? You know 16 plus options, so here's your challenge regarding collaboration. I'm not expecting you to go out and create a whole event or project or anything like that just for the sake of practicing collaborating. But I want you to look at what you already have going on in your life and think, how you can collaborate with at least one other person to make this thing happen. Just look at everything you're working on and see if any of these apply:

- Hire someone to support you in something.
- Get some mentorship advice on another thing you're working on.
- If you're trying to lose weight, and you know somebody else who is too, then work together on it.
- Is there anywhere else in your personal or professional life that you'd like to bring in collaboration?

I'm going to make this really simple. Collaborate with one other person in your professional or your personal life and then share with us on the Dynamic You™ Community how it's going. Feel free to share from the beginning what you want to collaborate on, and then share your progress and discoveries.

How Was The Challenge?

Chantal Staaf, "The collaboration one for me also was a fairly 'easy' one. I collaborate in both my personal and business life often. I do find that at times I am the giver, and have a harder time taking help. I have had to get better at this. My girlfriend and I work together to get kids to dance. Two more friends take my other daughter to cheer. It's give and take. In the business sense, I lend out my stock for my team to do events, I plan calls with other women/leaders on my team. I did find it particularly interesting about the 7 secrets. I have a large problem being honest about things not going well as I don't want to hurt feelings; however, the last few times things have gone sideways, I realized that had I mentioned something sooner, the problem/issue could have been avoided."

Sandra Girard, "In my day job I already have to collaborate with many different people all the time, whether it is meetings or planning for other events. In my personal life and my Rodan & Fields business, I am always collaborating. This is what I enjoy the most. Sometimes too much, as I often find myself stretched, but it is all the things that I want to be involved in, that is the challenge when it comes to balance."

Melody Owen, "To name a few things that I do where I collaborate with others; I work with others in a mastermind group, I collaborated on a conference this year, and run a group of authors. I see collaboration as part of building community, and connecting with others. So much more can be done when we work together, we can build bigger and better events, products, networks and we are all enriched in the process."

Cora Naylor, "I can see a lot of possibilities to collaborate with my Accountability Coaching. I have been approached by a couple of ladies in Australia that are working on some training for direct sales/network marketing people, and they are looking for someone to do the accountability component, so that may be one. I look forward to working with others on possible projects, webinars or groups."

Claudine Pender, "I am very good at collaborating. I do not impose my ideas. I will say my opinion, but I don't mind going with what the majority wants, for example. Of course, if I am the expert in something then I will support my opinion with facts/experience, etc. I am good at collaboration. I prefer to DIVIDE TASKS. I don't need two people doing the same job, I find it a waste of time. I am also good at reporting back and saying what I have done. A great example of collaboration was buying my first investment property with my friend Kika. She is married to my ex- husband. (By the way, me and my ex are GREAT at collaboration. We put our son's well being above anything else and we managed to raise him and make all big decisions together without fighting.) About the house! Kika and I worked very well and basically chose EVERYTHING together from the place to buy the house, the kind of house, the renovation, and the furniture. We were even complimented by the IKEA sales person when we bought a whole kitchen in two hours. The lady said buying an IKEA kitchen is a challenge and can ruin friendships and marriages. We survived! Oh, and we loaded my CRV and took it to the Sunshine Coast and unloaded it! Just writing this makes me think we really ARE GREAT FRIENDS AND TROOPERS!!! I can go on and on about collaboration. I love helping people so I collaborate a lot and people help me, too."

Tazeem Jamal, "I LOVE collaborating with others! It's the easiest way to connect with others that can benefit both parties! When I see a new business has opened in my community, I love to introduce myself and see if there is a way to help support them. In turn this can help to build my business. An example, I have been established in my Spa business for well over 27 years, when a new Float Spa opened, I introduced myself to the owner. I invited him to collaborate for our Holiday Open House and he agreed. We had some great door prizes, a lucky client of mine won the float experience and we used our clients and Social Media to promote them!"

CHAPTER 9
PILLAR 8: BE CONFIDENT

You are doing such a great job reading the Dynamic You™ book. In the first few Pillars we built the foundation of a Dynamic Woman™, and then in the next few Pillars we looked at other ways to dive inward and how to bring others in closer. Now, we will take it up a notch, the next two Pillars might feel a bit harder or even more exciting and enticing—you choose your perspective! I invite you right now, step into these last two Pillars, Pillar Eight and Pillar Nine.

Pillar Eight is all about being confident. Dynamic Women™ are confident, and if they aren't at first, they fake it until they make it. You want to be in a place where you are confident in every area of your life and in every situation. I know that's not going to be the case for a lot of us. I don't feel confident in every single moment, but what I'm going to give you today are seven ways we kill and zap away our own confidence. Then, I'm going to give you seven solutions for being more confident.

I want you to think right now. What is your initial reaction to the announcement of this Pillar? Some of the ladies in my program reacted this way:

- "Awesome, this is so important."
- "At first I thought Eeek! But I know it's something to work on."
- "It's always something you're striving for."
- "There are many layers to confidence and hearing you break them down was really helpful."
- "You are often in stages of confidence in a specific role, such as in being a parent. You can start to be confident with your baby and then she hits the terrible twos. It's a constant cycle of mastering where you are, being confident, then you get into a new stage and start all over, feeling like you're a novice in your confidence."

I have some other questions for you:

- Do you believe yourself to be a confident person? It's a yes or no. Yes? No?
- If you're thinking that sometimes you feel confident and other times you don't, give yourself a score out of 100%. What percentage of time are you confident? I want you to share your answer on the Dynamic You™ Global Community. Ex. I am confident 80% of the time or 25% of the time. Whatever your number is share it.

Being confident as a Dynamic Woman™ is so important that many of the Pillars won't work otherwise. For example, being magnetic and having charisma requires confidence. We want to make sure that this Pillar is strong for you.

You might be thinking, "Oh, I'm not a confident person," but having confidence in yourself isn't necessarily something you're born with. Confidence is something that you can build. You can increase your confidence. It's really just a state of mind, and if you really work on the little tricks I give you, you too can grow a kind of confidence that will be evident in every situation. That's 100% of the time AND in every area of your life. Sound good?

What I want you to do first is stop comparing yourself to everyone else. I want you to think of yourself and how awesome you are, especially because you have already learned the other seven Pillars, and I know you've been putting them into practice. Also, you are doing great things in your life. So, we are not going to catch compare-itis. We are not going to suffer from comparing and judging and all the consequences that follow. I want us to be in this place of self-confidence.

Confidence, Not Ego

On the other end of the spectrum, I'm guessing you don't want to have too much confidence, where it turns into arrogance or the ego taking control. I mentioned my Dynamic Power™ Program where I talked about **Power Over** and **Power Under**, and having too much confidence is one of those things that can put you in power over. A lack of confidence puts you in power under. I want us to think about being in that **Personal Power Sweet Spot™**, and apply that logic to a confidence sweet spot. When I teach my clients what their Personal Power Sweet Spot™ is, they gain confidence for being in that place because they see the results.

I'm going to take you through ways of building your confidence, but not to the extreme of arrogance. We know that Dynamic Women™ are not arrogant and they do not allow their egos to run the show. They are both humble and confident. They stand strong in knowing who they are, what they can provide and offer, and Dynamic Women™ stand up for themselves.

7 Ways We Kill Our Own Confidence

1. Procrastination and Perfectionism

Killer of confidence number one is procrastination and perfectionism, because these two evil "Ps" go hand in hand. Often, we procrastinate because we don't know how to do something, because we are scared of doing something, or because we don't want to do something. The other reason we procrastinate is because we think that whatever we do should be perfect. We want it to be perfect and so we don't move forward out of fear of being less than perfect. Total killer of confidence when you are procrastinating and when you are focusing on perfectionism.

The Solutions to Procrastination and Perfectionism

I can offer a couple of solutions to procrastination and perfectionism. If you hang out with people who are doers, if you hang out with people who don't procrastinate and people who don't suffer from perfectionism, it will rub off on you. You can talk to them. You can follow them. You can hang out with them. Being around them is going to give you confidence to step forward to do things, and doing things means you are not procrastinating. You are going to use them as role models. You are going to ask them for advice. You can look up to them for inspiration. Keep them around you because they are a better role model for you than someone who always procrastinates or is a perfectionist.

Make sure in your group of five that you include some people who show their confidence by stepping forward, even into things they don't know how to do. If you want to overcome the tendency to strive for perfectionism, you need to start valuing results that are less than perfect.

I mentioned how perfectionists compare themselves to others, but the problem is worse if they're merely beginners and are comparing themselves to those who are years ahead. It's an unfair benchmark, and you'll never match the expectation of being at a level you can't possibly be at given the lack of time and experience. If you do feel like you need to compare yourself to others for research purposes, do it with somebody who is at your same level or just a step ahead of you, not someone who is so much further ahead because all you're going to do is judge yourself.

Compare yourself to others by asking,

- What are my competitors doing?
- What's that person doing?
- Or I met this person who's working the same position as me, how can I learn from what she is doing?
- What are the people ahead of me doing? Do I like it? And if yes, how can I bring that in over the next six months to a year?

Additionally, do something you've been procrastinating. That's your homework. Is there something on your to-do list you have avoided for a long time? Do it, even if you don't possess all the tools, even if you don't know everything, just do it. If you really need to know something in order to get it done, then figure it out, because a lot of the time we procrastinate because we just don't know what the next step is. Let me know on the Dynamic You™ Global Community one thing you've been procrastinating that you are actually going to do.

2. Overwhelm

Killer of confidence number two, you are overwhelmed. So many things in your life, so many things to do, your schedule is full. You have no time and you have so many things going on and everything is so big. Life is overwhelming. So where do you even start? If you have been in that situation, you know how it can kill your confidence. When you're overwhelmed you're not in your brilliance. Instead, you are worrying about getting things done and you're in that place of lack, not enough time or energy or money or whatever it is.

Sandra says that being overwhelmed is the number one confidence-killer she faces. The trouble is we expect so much of ourselves every moment of every day. We over-schedule, we don't make time for ourselves. We don't eat, we don't exercise, relax or sleep enough. We run ourselves into the ground because the expectations we have of ourselves are so high. More often than not, it's a super long list that no one could ever get done, then we have low expectations of ourselves long-term. Instead, we need to lower the daily expectations we have for ourselves, and raise the overall expectations for our life. I say this because when I ask people what their plan for the day is, and then the plan for their life, the day list is often longer.

The Solutions to Overwhelm

Instead of being in that overwhelming place, you need to create a plan, a plan that has a step-by-step guide illustrating what you're going to do to get moving. The trouble is we schedule in projects rather than tasks. All you need to do is take the first step. You don't need to worry about 20 steps from now. Take the first step, complete a small task. It will build your confidence so that you know, "Okay, I'm not overwhelmed focusing on all the things I must do, instead, I'm focusing on only the next step and the next step and the next step." Soon, if you learn to work like this all the time, every time you make one of those small steps you build trust in yourself, trust that you can make big goals happen. Big things happen in my life just by taking it all one step at a time.

Another solution for being overwhelmed is to do small tasks and small things every day. They add up to a lot of accomplishments. Another solution you can do is set a small goal and achieve it. Rather than focusing on merely small tasks, actually break something into a smaller goals. If you set a goal of losing 20 pounds, why don't you just start with a goal of losing one? If you set the goal of being healthier, why don't you just focus on drinking eight glasses of water a day first? Set that as your goal. Set a small achievable goal. You don't have to take everything on at one time. You don't have to take on the world in one day.

Some questions to check in with yourself are:

- Am I being realistic with what I want to accomplish today?
- What are my top three priorities of what I need to accomplish?
- What structures need to be in place so I can do them?
- How am I going to celebrate after I accomplish them?
- What structures need to be in place next time to do this better?

If you are working on boosting your confidence, you need to choose something you know you can and will achieve. I remember working with a client who kept making these outrageous goals. Each goal was more difficult than the last and she set too many of them. She felt defeated by the end of the year because she didn't fully achieve any of her goals. Of course she didn't because other amazing opportunities arose and she ended up wanting to do other things. She didn't re-evaluate her goals and she still kept them big and out of reach. At the end of the year, she thought, "I'm a loser. I didn't do all these things." If she had just been a little more realistic in what she wanted to accomplish, and acknowledged all those other things that she did accomplish, then she would have been in a better place.

You can also give yourself time after you complete a task to let your mind wander. This helps you to process what you went through and be more productive moving forward. When people pack their day with no downtime, the mind waits for some quiet time to process the day. If the mind doesn't get this time to reflect, it will often choose some of the worst times to attempt to process things. For example, when you need to focus on an important task, when you're trying to relax at the spa, or when you're in your bed at night and trying to fall sleep.

The last solution to not being overwhelmed is just change one small habit. Maybe you can go to bed earlier. Maybe you can wake up earlier. Maybe you will journal or write down five points of gratitude, stop smoking, or stop eating so much sugar. Just say I am going to do this one little thing. Just one little thing for 30 days. And stick to that. I know there's the idea of the 100-day challenge, but just pick one small thing, one small habit and change that one small habit. That is going to boost your confidence. The more you commit to something, follow through and do it, the more you will trust yourself to make even more goals and follow through with them as well.

3. Negative Self-Talk

Killer of confidence number three, negative self-talk. We discussed this a little when we learned about the saboteur. What I want you to focus on now is not just negative self-talk, but also stopping your negative thoughts.

The Solution to Negative Self-Talk and Negative Thoughts

The solution is getting to know yourself. When you get to know yourself and listen to your thoughts rather than smother them, you stop worrying. You actually start processing. This just happened with a client of mine the other day. She is just so busy. She doesn't make time in her day to actually process what she is going through. The result is she can't fall asleep at night and she wakes up in the middle of the night.

She says she can't get to sleep because her mind wanders at night. If she just acknowledged her thoughts in the moment throughout her day, her mind wouldn't need to try to process things at night when she should be sleeping. Previously we discussed setting your alarm to be more self-aware in changing your perspective. If you can get to know yourself in a deep way, your inner dialogue would sound something like this: "Hmm. Ah, I react this way in this situation" or "I don't like that I did this" or "I don't really possess these skills." The more you can just make your self-observations facts, rather than emotional based judgements, the more you remove yourself and then start to think and act positively.

I know I shared with you before how thinking positively changes you because your beliefs become your thoughts, which become your words, which become your actions and then the reactions of others. I not only want you to be thinking positively, but also acting positively. What does that look like for you?

The last solution for negative self-talk is to focus on exactly that—the solution. Rather than focusing on the problem, complaining and whining, focus on the solution to the problem. Yes, you need to be able to identify the problem first. But once you do, shift your focus from the problem or the obstacle and onto the solution. Don't think, "Oh, my gosh, it's raining," and stop there. Get your umbrella out: problem solved. You're not going to get wet now.

Make changes based on the solution. Don't make changes based on the problem. Rather than saying, "Oh, my gosh, I'm so tired," do something to solve it. Go to bed early. "Oh, my kids are bothering me." What do they want? Some connection with you? Some time with you? Make that happen. Look to the how can I. How can I solve this problem? How can I start liking something I don't like? How can I change that thing around which I'm having negative self-talk? Ask yourself, what's the solution? How can I make it better?

4. Feeling Small around Others

The number four killer of your confidence is feeling small around others. A little case of the old compare-itis. I'm sure you've been there and can relate. I'm going to give you some really great solutions.

Solutions to Feeling Small

One way you can feel more confident is by dressing the part. Dress to impress. If you have your hair done and accessories on and nice clothes, I'm not saying you need to go and buy the most expensive clothes, I'm not saying that by any means. The key point is you need to feel confident in the clothes that you are wearing. You should be dressing for the level of success and confidence that you want. You'd never show up at a grand event wearing your jeans. So always make sure you show up wearing something that makes you feel good, because that will come across to others.

Second is stand tall, focus on your posture. Posture says so much non-verbally about your confidence. Often you will see people who roll their shoulders forward, making them appear as though they're smaller, or even trying to make themselves disappear. Even if the person is smiling or outgoing, you can sense something is off. It changes your perception of them. A little trick is to throw your shoulders up as high as they will go, roll them back and drop them.

Try doing it now if you haven't already. Do it again. Shoulders up, roll back, drop, and make sure those girls are out. You know what I mean, stick out your chest. That immediately changes your posture. In comparison, when your posture is poor, you exhibit lower self-esteem, lower self-confidence, and you are not in a powerful stance. Also, having your arms at your sides or moving and open when you talk is better than crossed arms.

I have noticed a lot of people place their hands behind their backs when they stand to ask questions, or are at a microphone, or are introducing themselves. Standing with your hands behind your back is a victim stance, a stance of service and servitude. Please do not do that. Instead place your arms at your sides. Again, shoulders up, roll them back, drop, and make sure the girls are out and your chin is straight. But we don't want our chin up in the air, because remember, we are not trying to portray a large ego or arrogance. When you are talking to someone, make sure you maintain eye contact with her. Looking a person in the eye shows confidence. I know in certain cultures, because I lived in Japan for three years and worked for a Korean Company for six, I learned pretty quickly some cultures don't look you straight in your eyes unless they are an equal or higher up than you in a hierarchy. So don't take it personally if they avoid eye contact with you.

But in the Western World, looking people in the eye is a sign of respect, respect for them and respect for yourself. Choose to look people in the eyes rather than looking down at your shoes, or looking beyond their face. That's not showing confidence. Yes, it's sometimes uncomfortable to stare at somebody the whole time we're talking, and you don't want to maintain such strict eye contact that it feels strange. We naturally look away briefly and think for a second, but make sure your eyes meet theirs again and again each time you look away. Eye contact creates connection and that connection displays confidence because you are willing and able and confident enough to be seen.

Another thing you can do to show you are confident is to speak slowly. When you speak slowly, people listen to what you are saying because you make it seem more important. You are using pauses to highlight the important words. If I was standing on stage, I could use a slower pace as a way of pulling in the audience and getting them to lean in and listen a little bit closer. When I'm on video, my goal is to be highly engaging and ooze high energy because I've already built a rapport with my viewers. On video I'm trying to pack a lot of information into one sitting and share it as quickly as possible because your ears and your brain are processing it all a lot faster than if I was to speak slowly. Another tip is by speaking fast it makes sure you are not multitasking. By speaking faster, I know that I have your attention a little bit more than speaking slowly. That often happens with a lot of people who are extremely intellectual. They will speak slowly because they are downloading what they are thinking and they are saying it in a specific way. Try it out, see how that works for you.

Here is the last solution regarding feeling small around others. I hate over edited images, and I think people should just look how they really are. But I have an analogy for you. Imagine how life would be if you could just Photoshop your own self-image. I have recently experienced this in a positive way and in a negative way. I wanted to share how I feel about myself and my self-image and what I learned about that.

If you have followed me or attended my live events over the past six months to a year, you probably noticed that I've recently lost weight. I lost 40 pounds by doing a clean-eating program, one that I'm now teaching because I believe in it so much. Anyway, I found that I put on a lot of weight when I had my children. I'm part of the population who didn't lose weight while I nursed, and it was really important to me to be able to nurse as long as I could, so the extra weight just sat on me. Every now and again, I'd see a photo of myself and go, "Oh, my goodness. I didn't realize I looked like that." Once I saw the photo, I realized I was a lot bigger than my own mental image of myself. While it was really good for me to maintain a very positive self-image, I didn't like how heavy I actually was.

It worked out well for me that I felt a lot thinner than I actually was—the proof was in the picture I saw. Maybe you have had one of those cases where you see a photograph of yourself and you were surprised by how you looked. Since my self-image was very positive, I was still able to walk into the world confidently. But after seeing more images of myself larger than I had thought, my positive self-image began to turn into a negative one.

Then, I lost 40 pounds within six months. I feel proud of that, but the problem was my negative self-image didn't change because it was such a quick drop of weight my mind didn't believe it. Then I had a photoshoot, and when I went to look at the gallery I saw my full silhouette, and I thought, "Oh, my gosh. That's how I look now! I'm thinner than I thought!" Even though I was skinnier for months, I had to wait until I saw another full-length photo to truly change my self-image of myself. (Curious about which photos? Just look at them through the book and on the cover.)

Rather than rushing off to look at photos of yourself, I want you to say right now how you feel about your body. How do you feel about the way you present yourself? Is it positive or is it negative? You are a beautiful person and you should see yourself that way. So how would it be if you could create the best self-image of yourself? Carry the most positive self-image?

Do this by focusing on what you love. If you walk through life with the new and improved positive version of yourself in your mind, that image is going to raise your confidence. When you get around others, you are going to be able to stand in your confidence. Know that, yes, if you really don't like your self-image for a good reason, you can change it in a healthy way, like with a new hair cut, or how I ate clean, but then that's up to you and not others. Instead of putting your energy into what you don't like, put your energy into figuring out how to love yourself, not into how you don't like it as is.

5. Feel like a Fraud

The killer of confidence number five is that you feel unqualified or you feel like a fraud. I hear that a lot when women talk about starting their own business. A lot of times we feel under qualified or that we are frauds, but we just have to own where we are in our situation. If you are starting out a business and you go to an event where people are further ahead of you, just own that you are new, don't try to fake experience. Experience you can gain as you go along.

Three Solutions so You Don't Feel like a Fraud

Be Prepared

If you're telling yourself, "Oh, I'm new to this whole business thing," make sure you at least know how to explain what you do and what you are looking for. Spend some time with that. If you are going to enter a panel where you will to be asked questions, be prepared for how you are going to answer. It might take a little bit more learning. Remember the first time you drove a car? It felt like, "Okay, I need to put the car into gear, I need to check the rear-view mirror, I need to check the side mirror and over my shoulder before switching lanes." Every part of it felt awkward and you had to remind yourself of what to do step by step. But the more time you spent driving and as the years passed by, all these things eventually became so natural they are now second nature. The more you prepare yourself the more confident and automatic it becomes.

Increase Your Experience

When you're more experienced you're going to feel like you fit in more. You are going to feel like you earned it. Do you feel unqualified? What is it you feel unqualified about? I just talked about my weight loss journey, I felt like in order for me to teach it, I really had to have more practice with it. So I studied under two different professionals with two different modalities and I was able to blend them together. I became experienced in what I wanted to know. I read more and I studied. Then I practiced. I practiced on myself. I then practiced it on others and they achieved great results too. Figure out what you need to work on. Write it down, ask yourself questions, and then become more proficient in using the skills that are needed to make it happen.

Become More Knowledgeable

Empower yourself with knowledge. When you are prepared, you have the experience, and you have the knowledge, you are unshakable. You can stay in the competency. Just work on presenting it or discussing it or sharing it or whatever you are doing with the information. Maybe you need to go on the Internet and learn more. Maybe you need to actually hire somebody to teach you. Maybe you just need to read more books. Whatever you need to do, do it. Learn more so that when you speak, you know that what you are saying is correct.

6. Scared of Failure and Success

Sometimes people are scared of doing something because it is new. Is that you? Are you scared of the next big step or are you scared because you don't know what the next step is? I hear this so many times.

When you are afraid of success you're not being afraid of achieving great results, you're afraid of what great results will do to you, who you are as a person, your values, your relationships, your priorities, and your life.

People don't walk around saying, "I'm afraid of having lots of money, I'm scared of having ideal clients, I'm fearful of finding the right partner." It's more like, "I'm afraid the money is going to change me, I'm scared that because of all of the success all the people around me won't love me anymore."

Angela asked, "How can we know if we have a fear of success?" When I asked the ladies going through the program to put their hands up if they have a fear of success, more than half went up.

Solutions to Fear of Failure and Success

Instead of focusing on being scared of failure and scared of success, just focus on the next step, on completing the task. Focus on getting yourself closer to reaching your goal. As you go along the path, your confidence in completing each step will get you ready for this part.

I was the keynote speaker at a massive conference in the States. Lots of people, over 300 women attended. That could have seemed pretty scary when I was accepted, but I just focused on one step at a time. In the beginning I told myself, "I haven't done all the preparation, all the planning, all the knowledge seeking, all the competency training to prepare yet, so I'm not thinking about standing on stage yet. I'm thinking about what I will be delivering and how I'll deliver it. And then, I'm going to practice my delivery." As you do each step, and as you are successful at each little step, you'll feel confident doing that step again. If we talk about business, the first time you pick up the phone to cold call somebody is scary. But the second time will be a little less scary. Over time, you kind of look back and you go, "Why was I ever nervous about that? That was so easy. I'm a pro now."

Don't be afraid of receiving "no" for an answer. Instead of fearing answers and what will happen if you don't do everything just right, fear doing nothing at all. Just sitting there and doing nothing sucks, it's terrible, and it's going to kill your confidence. Don't let failure be the focus of your fears. Failure is part of the learning process. Everyone fails at some point, especially the most successful people in the world. Take the word "failure" out of your vocabulary, because if you give that to your saboteur, they are just going to run with it. Never give up. Again, failure is not an option. Don't accept failure. Think now, there's a solution to this. What's the solution? What's the solution to get past this obstacle? If your first idea for a solution doesn't work, ask yourself, well, what's my solution to that? As you succeed, you'll learn that adversity will always co-exist with challenge. When you learn to anticipate obstacles and also anticipate your success in the face of obstacles, there's going to be an even bigger boost of confidence that comes.

7. Being Indecisive

The last killer of confidence is being indecisive, going with somebody else's opinion or sticking with the majority even though you oppose. When you don't trust yourself and you place yourself in a position where you give in and go with what someone else wants, you come in that power under position and anyone in power over is going to be able to take advantage of you. You can also sit in limbo, telling yourself, "Maybe I should do this or maybe I should do that or maybe I should do that." I've seen this in clients when they are like, "I'm going to do this. I'm going to do this and this and this and this and this because I can't just decide on one." If you are trying to do everything, or you just can't decide because you're too worried you'll make the wrong choice, you are not going to get very far.

Solutions to Being Indecisive

I encourage you to get past this by being assertive. Stand up for what you believe. Stick to your principles. Choose a path and stay on it. Stay the course. If the path changes, that's okay, but then you stand in that new way with confidence. Flexibility is important because people change their minds all the time. Life is full of change. I change my mind when I see that something is not optimal, whether it's in my personal life or a business decision. Maybe I changed, or maybe it was my circumstances that changed. If you change, stand in that. Don't let anyone change you back to how it was before if you truly believe in this new way. Know your values and live with them.

I run a program called Dynamic Balance™ where we go through your values and priorities to create dynamic goals in every area of your life. The clients I work with one-on-one know values are important. I don't mean morals; I mean your values. Your confidence comes when you stand true and stay true to what you believe. One time I was in line to make a purchase in a store and I noticed the person ahead of me shoplifting. I couldn't just standby and keep it to myself because I knew that this was a charity shop. The money raised was for charity. Even if it wasn't for charity, I couldn't standby. In line, I'm watching this happen. I was shocked it was happening, and I was even more shocked that even though others could see as well, no one was saying anything to the cashier who was too busy to notice. The shoplifter put some items on the counter, but because the counter was so high, she was able to slip other items that she hadn't paid for into her bag.

I was standing there thinking, "What do I do?" I knew that if I didn't say anything, this would just haunt me for the rest of the day or the week or for a long time. I made eye contact with the person, and standing in my confidence, I said, "I see what you are doing." I didn't say, "You are shoplifting. Stop it." I said, "I see what you are doing." I gave her the opportunity to fix it. She didn't admit to it and so I said, "Okay, I see what you are doing. I see you are putting things in your bag as you put things on the counter." No one spoke up. No one said anything. No one backed me up. At that point, I could have just backed down and apologized for bothering her.

When in your life have you wished you could stand up a little bit stronger? When in your life have you stood up strong to somebody else because something wasn't right? Just think of how important that was to you. With my story in the shop, in that moment it was important to me that I stood up and I said something. She did actually admit she 'accidently' put a few things in her bag, and so she pulled them back out and put them on the counter to pay for them. When she left, I told the cashier, "I had to say something." He silently mouthed to me, "Thank you."

But the people behind me said, "You don't know their situation." I got a lot of flak for speaking up, but I knew I needed to say something. Stand up for what you believe. Stand up for what is right and wrong. Don't just stand up for other people, stand up for yourself. If something is not right, stand up for yourself. It doesn't mean that you have to be angry or yell. Get into your confidence pose and make eye contact. Speak slowly if you need to and come from that place of, "These are my values and these are my guidelines and my priorities and I'm standing strong in them."

I did have to go and chat with her because my curiosity and empathy kicked in. Was she really struggling? Could she not afford the items? Did she need help? Though she still denied stealing, a little chat outside as she smoked a cigarette confirmed I had done the right thing.

Birds of a Feather Flock Together

Generally speaking, people are attracted to others who are confident. If you want to be confident, hang around people who are confident. Let it rub off on you and you will attract people who want to be around you because of your confidence. I just want to share one more thing. Have you ever seen a speaker on stage who you knew was super nervous and you felt for her? Maybe you actually stopped listening to her message because your heart was just going out to her and wanting her to succeed and wanting her to not be so nervous.

Think about how you feel when you are around somebody who you know isn't confident. It's the same feeling. You struggle to listen to her message because you're too busy worrying about how she is feeling. We all want to be standing in our full confidence.

Here Is Your Challenge

What I want you to do is create a great list. An "I'm Awesome List". An "I'm dynamic for these reasons list." For this challenge, you are going to come up with 100 reasons why you're awesome. You can focus on actions, skills, experiences, ways of being, and things that you have actually accomplished.

I want to check in. How are you feeling right now about coming up with that list of 100? Did your brain go, "Oh, my gosh, that's too many! I could never complete that!"? Negative self-talk. What did your saboteur say? "I don't think I have achieved that many things compared to others." Are you coming down with compare-itis? What has happened? Did you sink into yourself and lose your good posture? What is it? Were you judging yourself? Did it just feel overwhelming? Did any of these seven killers come into play as you read this challenge?

Your goal is to create a list of 100 things that make you awesome. Reasons why you are awesome and do it on your own first. Come back to it a couple of times and then ask others to fill in the blanks. If there are any leftover blanks, you ask others, "Can you tell me why I'm awesome? Can you tell me why I'm great? Can you tell me what I've achieved?"

Here are some examples from some of my clients:

Cora – I'm an awesome at brainstorming.

Pam – I'm awesome with details.

Claire – I'm tenacious.

Melody – I'm good at giving credit to others.

Maria – I'm positive.

Sukeina – I'm good at organizing events.

Fatima – I'm passionate.

Sandra – I'm awesome at the fine details.

Michelle – I'm awesome at collaborating

Claudine – I'm awesome because I'm eager to learn.

Angela – I can relate to many different people.

Leagh – I'm intelligent.

Tazeem - I am awesome because I am a connector.

If you're stuck and are having a hard time making a list of 100 reasons why you are awesome, start with any of your big achievements, then go on to smaller accomplishments that came along the way. Ask yourself what helped me get there? Then you'll see some of the other reasons why you're awesome! Here are some ideas that came from the a client's big achievement of, "I closed 20 large deals this year."

- I wrote a sales script
- I became more comfortable making cold calls
- I'm good at some new sales techniques
- I'm a master at follow-up
- I'm organized
- I'm creative

Your list of 100 reasons why you're awesome is now a great way to boost motivation, build future confidence and give you creative ways of getting better results in the future.

That's the end of the seven killers of confidence. I would love for you to stand in the seven solutions, the seven ways to boost your confidence over the next week. Let me know what works. Let me know your experiences, which ones are easy for you, which ones are a little bit harder, and don't forget to ask for support.

How Was The Challenge?

Angela Foran, "I feel confident 80% of the time. I think my two top confidence killers are indecision and procrastination. My whole life I have been indecisive in almost all areas. I have gotten better since having a child, since who has time to contemplate options when you are trying to get things done during naptime.

"Also when I really, really want to do something, I am not indecisive at all and will not procrastinate, if anything I might jump in too quickly. I will typically put off things I don't like to do, they actually might not even make it onto my to-do list, or they just get passed over for other easier or more enjoyable things."

Anneliese Dusseldorf, "Pillar #8 is by far the toughest one. The Killer of Confidence I struggle with the most is fear of success. Growing up with a physical challenge, I was continually told I couldn't do a lot of things as my parents and teachers were afraid I would get injured, which has led to me being afraid of true success. A big part of why I have my business is to show myself and others that I can be successful in my business."

Cora Naylor, "I wanted to share a "success." I put my "confident" face on at an event this week called the "Dare to Dream Soiree," and [I] met some amazing ladies at the event! I ended up booking three Accountability Sessions from that evening! (Two with people I already knew and one with a doctor I met that evening) I also got some great feedback about my new business from a few others. I'm excited!!!

Leagh Wright, "I have two killers that really resonated with me: Procrastination and Overwhelm. I think the two are connected for me. I get overwhelmed and thus procrastinate. So I bit the bullet this week on a few things and just did it. They weren't as bad as I thought they might be. I'm also checking in with myself regularly too. To stay on the path I need to be on. It's so easy to get off course again. Thank You!"

Claire Madin, "This week I have had to bring my confidence with organizing the first trek for West Women Trekkers™ that's happening next week. I have often had an issue with being confident enough to share and promote myself or what I am achieving. In the past, I have liked to continue under the radar and complete different tasks successfully along the way. As a new solopreneur, this has had to change, as I am now the face, marketer, promoter of what I do and what I can contribute. This is a work in progress, but I feel I am moving closer towards this goal with small steps, such as videos on Facebook, Instagram and marketing tools."

Claudine Pender, "I feel confident 80% of the time. Which of the solutions are harder? #3, negative self-talk [and] #1, procrastination—things that are harder are "pushed" away. [And] #2, overwhelmed—sometimes there is too much and I get paralyzed. But then I make a plan and get things done little by little. I tend to get overwhelmed because I want to do a lot. I have been told before I have fear of success. I find that interesting because I know that fear of failure doesn't stop me."

Leagh Wright, "Confidence is such an interesting topic. It is so relevant in all aspects of our lives. I'm glad this one came up. I am generally quite confident, probably 80% of the time. I am new in mortgages, commercial and construction are daunting because of their complexities, but I have the best partner for this, which is comforting. I am definitely not alone. I struggled with confidence and feeling like I belonged for the first while in my career changes. It was a major transformation for me, but that has since been greatly improved. As for a confidence killer I would say procrastination and poor time management has been my detriment. I am conscious of this and am really working at it.

"My second area for improvement is my network. I really need to improve my inner circle of close friends; I have grown out of some old ones. That is also improving. So I am quite grateful for how things are changing and improving.

Pam Karlen, "My confidence is at an 80%. My confidence Killers are overwhelm & procrastination. Also when I get in a crowd where I think people know more than I do I can find myself shrinking into a corner."

Chantal Staaf, "I am confident... hmmm not really, I am going with probably 40-50 % of the time and yet I have some much to be confident about - this is one of the primary reasons I joined this program. I remember once I did an Epicure party and a really successful woman was there, she looked at me and said WOW you are so confident, and I remember looking at her like yeah right and then I realized that I am most confident in my business. I feel like I can be myself and everyone accepts me for who I am. I too am guilty of quite a few of the killers, overwhelm for sure! I have too much going on and I do it to myself. Not sure why really, except for it dawned on me fairly recently that I do so much for other so that I can feel worthy of their time/ energy/ love etc.

"I have been really working hard on my negative self-talk - OH YEAH BABY!! It's probably the highest for me. Despite me shutting that saboteur up she seems to weasel her way back. Now that she is on my radar though, I find if I talk out loud to myself she gets scared and runs off.

"Feeling small around others is another big one, I find I put people on a pedestal which makes me feel small. I'm working on this one too especially because you gave us the homework of writing a list of how awesome I am.

"I am scared of failure/success. I wonder what would my life look like if I didn't 'need' so and so person because I'm so successful - kind of scary."

Cora Naylor, My confidence score is 70%. I am mostly confident, but there are some areas that come along and hold me back. Procrastination is a killer of mine mostly with learning new things or taking time to "make a plan". Something I am definitely in the process of improving is negative self-talk. It happens if I'm not doing the activities I need to do.

"I can also feel unqualified. I'm working on overcoming it as this wants to come out while I'm launching my new Accountability Coaching business. In a way I feel like a Jekyll/Hyde inside my head. I know I can do it, but there is the doubter niggling away there. I need to starting my 100 list today!"

Melody Owen, "My biggest confidence killer is overwhelm. I find myself afraid to commit to anything big just in case chaos and crisis take over my life. I have had too much on my plate for the past few years, and as I come out of that stage of my life, I struggle with the fear that it isn't over yet. For example, tomorrow is my mother's annual care conference. (My mother has had Alzheimer's for about 15 years and I have been her main family caregiver the entire time, taking on all the emotional and physical burden by myself. She is now in a home, which helps.)

"At this point in the journey, just showing up to her home feels overwhelming and soul crushing and so this week will be challenging. I will take the morning off and just look after me to deal with the emotional and physical overload it takes to show up and have meaningful conversations with her caregivers. My mantra in these moments is that I am just one person and can only do what I can do. I say that to myself and other people when they expect things of me as well. Some people see this as an excuse, which I have learned to use to evaluate their place in my life. That [being] said, I am aching to lift these overwhelming responsibilities off my shoulder and live for myself. I know that I have more time available than I did a few years ago, but I am not living that way fully yet. There is much work to do in this area.

"Where do I do well in the confidence Pillar?

- I am decisive. I make decisions quite quickly and confidently.
- I love myself, treat myself gently and practice positive self-talk.
- I know that I am enough and do not feel small around others.

Sandra Girard, "I am confident 80% of the time. This one really spoke to me in so many ways—the 7 Killers of Confidence, especially procrastinate and overwhelmed! I find that when I am not confident or have the knowledge of something, I DO procrastinate. You asked us to do something that we have been procrastinating—I am not social media savvy and I have dabbled in Instagram, Twitter and Facebook. I am working with someone now who has the expertise in this area, and learning how to simplify it instead of overthinking and struggling with it. Baby steps and building off my confidence. When I am feeling overwhelmed, I often don't know where to start, so I start many things and don't feel like I am in my "brilliance." I will build trust in myself and take [it] one step at a time, and do one small thing every day. I liked the part about "dressing the part" and stand in your power. Amy Cuddy (social psychologist—one of the most watched TedX) says "body language affects how others see us." She talks about power posing and standing in a posture of confidence even when we don't feel confident. I am starting my 100 reasons I am awesome."

Claire Madin, "I am confident 60-70% of the time. This Pillar was very interesting. As it progressed, I felt like I was looking at a self-reflection that has been through each stage of the 7 killers of confidence! Procrastination TICK, Overwhelmed TICK, Negative Self Talk TICK, Feeling Small TICK, etc. These have been recurrent stages at one point or another in life. Confidence is definitely an ongoing work in progress theme for me! The primary example I can give is when I am new to something and set a high expectation. If asked a question, I will freeze and wait for someone else to answer, as I am scared to get the answer wrong. This has been apparent most recently with my personal trainer course, when I lack confidence I over think and make the process more complex than it needs to be. Diane saying, "OWN WHERE YOU ARE IN YOUR SITUATION" resonated with me profoundly. I will be implementing this in my role this week. I start training clients this week, and I am committing to being decisive, prepared, and excited for the success. I am going to own it. I have been procrastinating on social media with West Women Trekkers™ and finally completed a video last week to launch the date for our first North Shore hike. This was way beyond my comfort zone, but I got over it and posted in online to a resounding stream of positive feedback!"

If I was to put this as the first Pillar, how would your experience have been?

Are you like *Cora* who felt that, "It would have been harder to acknowledge having a lower confidence to others in the group if we had started with this Pillar." Or maybe like *Maria* who shared, "It would have killed my confidence if we leaded with this as the first Pillar. I benefitted more by having the other Pillars to warm me up."

The killer of *Maria's* confidence recently was overwhelm. She felt overwhelmed with doing prospecting calls and entering everyone in her new CRM. After we discussed it, we were able to bring in a few solutions. We created a system around it and structured it. We broke it down into a step-by-step plan that was manageable, so she had three calls a day. She did them first thing in the day, so it was like the eat the frog idea where you do your toughest/most important task of the day first, which also helps you to have more motivation throughout the rest of the day. It was a realistic plan and she had consistent results because we built a routine around it. Each day she did it her confidence grew, and now she likes talking to people and making the calls. She used to dread them and now she looks forward to them.

One of the saboteurs for *Claudine* is Cruella. She says, "You are not doing things properly. You're not doing enough. Everything you're doing, you should do better." When I asked her if she felt logically Cruella to be right, she gave a big sigh and then replied, "It hurts me when I don't do whatever Cruella wants me to do." Then I asked her if someone else looked at her life, would she think Cruella is right? AND she answered, "No! She thinks I accomplish a lot." So even though *Claudine* knows Cruella is wrong, she is driven to do more and never feel like she has done enough. The trouble with listening to Cruella and believing her is that *Claudine* judges herself and feels guilty, and she never gets the chance to celebrate because Cruella never pats her on the back.

Together we came up with some ways to get rid of Cruella:

- Cruella had to go read a book
- Cruella should go find some labour intensive job like sweeping so she was busy
- Cruella could clean the bathrooms and do the ironing

It was interesting to see how much lighter *Claudine* became from doing this activity. She was laughing and having fun! Now, before *Claudine* starts her day, she can send Cruella out to do one of these activities and you can do the same with your saboteur.

CHAPTER 10
PILLAR 9: SHINE

We are on the final Pillar. Wow, we've gone through eight Pillars, and now it's the last one. It's a little bittersweet, because if you've been sharing on the Community, then I've seen you grow, and change, and stretch, and challenge yourself through all the Pillars. Now is the final Pillar. Are you excited? Are you nervous? Are you sad? Just check in with yourself for a moment. What are you feeling now? There are no wrong feelings.

The last Pillar is actually a lovely combination of a bunch of the Pillars. Let me tell you what it is, and then I'll tell you how it's a blend of some of the others. I call this Pillar "Shining." In my head is that song by, Rihanna, "Shine bright like a diamond, shine bright like a diamond." Compare this Pillar to a diamond, consider how a diamond shines and sparkles. Consider what a diamond represents in our minds; i.e., high quality, high value, something people yearn for, something they're drawn to.

When *Tazeem* heard that this was the last Pillar, she thought, "Uh Oh! We have to talk about ourselves and share with the world how we shine." But it's a good thing because it pushes us to be more out there. Instead of worrying you only shine by talking about yourself, or even by being the life of the party, remember, shining is more about showing up fully as you are—and that can even happen in a one-on-one conversation. Everyone shines in her own way.

Start off by thinking of someone who stands out in your life, someone who you feel is always shining. Can you now feel what it's like to shine? It's a bit different than magnetic, where you feel drawn to them. When you're shining, you definitely attract people, but when you shine it is an outward action; meanwhile, being magnetic is focusing on pulling in. When you're shining, you're actually better able to fulfill your life purpose, and you're able to go for your dreams.

You are also going to feel more satisfied, and that's why I left it until last, because it's a little similar to presence, like I mentioned with confidence. But I use the word "shine" because it's more energetic. It's more dynamic than the word "presence".

It is a great blend, like I said, of a lot of the Pillars. Mainly, it pulls from connected, magnetic, and confident. There are different levels of shining. Shining is the ultimate level, but let me tell you all the different levels, and I want you to determine where you are. You might be at different levels in different areas of your life, so read through them and think, "Where am I in my career? And where am I with my friends? And where am I with my family?"

We all shine in different ways. So as you're reading them, please think about the way you shine and apply it to that. Going through them, I'll begin at the lower end and move my way up.

Six Levels of Shining

Level One: Hiding

Rather than being out and shining, you're staying home. You're holding back. You're keeping yourself in. And because you're hiding, you're not shining, really, at all.

Level Two: Invisible

You go out to things and you meet people when you reach out. Even though you are at events, and you do things, you're kind of invisible. You're not getting much attention, no one is paying much attention to you at all. Not much is happening from you or for you.

Level Three: Blending In

Yes, you're there, and yes, people know that you exist, but you're more or less just a body in the room. You're not putting anything out; you're not shining in any way that makes you different from anyone else. Imagine going to an event and everybody's wearing the same thing. Or in the wintertime how everyone likes to wear black, black on black, or navy blue and other dark neutrals. If we think of it in terms of your appearance, you merely blend in with everyone else, wearing the same uniform as them. Maybe you're too quiet. Maybe you don't speak up, or ask questions. That's blending in.

Level Four: You're Seen

At this level, we start to shine. If we have a neutral place on the scale, or a middle point, we are now past that and crossing into shine territory. If you are a level four, you're being seen. You show up, and people see you, and people know you're there, and people meet you. People may even get a feeling about you, but it's more of an external, shallow feeling. You're simply seen.

Level Five: Being Witnessed

If we go a little bit further towards fully shining, we are being witnessed. Being witnessed means you are not only seen, but you share, by communicating in one way or another. You share, and people get a greater understanding of who you are. You are discussing something. You grab a microphone and you ask a question. Or you are on stage discussing something and you open up a little bit more. When you are being witnessed, you're seen for some of the things that make you unique. You are seen in a way people can begin to appropriately define you and describe you to someone else.

If you think of somebody you have just seen around, maybe you've see her in various places or at select events. You see her, you see her, you see her, but you don't really know her. Maybe you speak with her, and then at the end, you think, "man, I thought she was one way, but now I know she's really another." Or "wow, I thought she would be egotistical because of all her success, but she is very humble." You get to peak under the hood and really see the underneath. That is what it's like when you witness someone else.

Level Six: Shining

We're at shining. What is shining? Shining is when you are there and you are yourself, you are noticed by people, and you are understood. Your deeper, inner self is seen by others. It's kind of hard when you go to some events and you don't really have the time to talk to anybody. Or if you host a party or a dinner, you don't have time to make those deep, one-on-one connections with your guests. I hate hosting parties because I feel like I just say, "Hi, how are you? How are you? How are you?" and I never get the chance to have profound conversations with people. I'm not even being witnessed, I'm just kind of buzzing around.

When you are shining, you are in your core competencies. These are the things you were destined to do. These are things you use to leave a legacy. People have said to me, "Oh, Diane, when I see you lead something, or you are onstage, or you're telling a story, or a joke or something, then that's when I really see who you are." A little while back a friend of mine posted a picture of herself smiling and beaming. Even though it was a fuzzy, grainy picture, I couldn't stop staring because I could see her spirit almost literally coming out. She said, "This is how I feel. This picture shows how I feel as a person." I said, "Yeah, and that's exactly how I see you." When you shine, people get the full essence of you.

Maybe you have a friend, someone you are close to, and when she's in her element you get to see her shine. You watch her step into the great person she is. It's kind of like you are in the moment, and in that moment, nothing can go wrong. People just want more of you, and they appreciate what you do. Shining has such a positive, powerful space in our lives.

Before I talk about the steps and the ways to shine brighter in your life, I want to ask a tough question. I gave you the six different levels—so where are you in those? Be honest. Are you being seen or are you hiding? Are you invisible or are you blending in? Where are you in the different areas of your life? Write that down first, if you haven't already, and then I want you to answer this next question. Pause if you want to write all this down, because I'm going to come back and I'm going to ask you a question, and I want you to have all your answers ready. I'm going to let you pause now.

Welcome back, I have another tough question for you. Based on where you are within those six levels, I want to ask you, are others doing this to you? If you're working for somebody else, are they pushing you down? If so, are they making you invisible? Is a partner, a friend, family members, are they doing this to you? Or are you doing this to yourself? There's no judgment either way, but the truth is, if others are doing it to you, you are permitting them to do it. You need to take control over your opportunities to shine. You need to take control over your ability to shine. I know you can. You have a huge purpose here on Earth. I trust we can move you towards that shining space.

Five Ways to SHINE More

Let me go through the five different ways you can increase your ability to shine. Are you ready?

1. Be Visible

What do I mean by "be visible?" Be out there and in person. Be alive at events, and be online. Have both. I'm not saying you need to accept every invitation and attend every event that comes your way. And I'm not suggesting you create an account for every existing social media platform. You just need to dabble, a little bit, in both. Put yourself out there.

Be where your people are. You are not going to be visible and enjoy shining in places where you don't feel you should be in the first place. And you're not going to be able to shine in places where your people aren't. "Your people" aren't necessarily exactly like you, they may be the complete opposite of you. Your people are the people who see you. Be with them. And so too, be in the places where you are visible.

Finally, make sure your appearance portrays the right message. Being visible doesn't mean you have to blend in. And it doesn't mean you have to venture way out there in your appearance—you don't want to be visible merely because you've got a little too much skin showing. We don't want that, but we want you to feel comfortable in your clothes, and be visible. You can wear the simple black dress, but maybe put a sparkly necklace on. What are other ways you can shine in your appearance? If you want to wear simple jeans and a t-shirt, that's fine too, but maybe wear a pair of killer heels. Or if heels aren't your thing, be bold and wear some colorful, hip sneakers. Think of a way you can highlight your uniqueness. Whether you are serious, glamorous, or you're playful, play up your personality and accentuate your individual style. The way in which you physically present yourself informs others about you. And if you're shining as your real, authentic self, your stylistic choices will never overpower and outshine who you are as a person. Just make sure you aren't hiding behind your appearance because you want to be able to connect with others as who you are not as what you wear. If you were to have crazy big hair, tons of makeup, all these wild clothes, and tons of bling and jewellery, and lots of colors and patterns, people see what you're wearing first and see you second. It's your job to make the choice, but my job to say it.

Since I often am in a professional setting doing a job, I need to make sure my outfit doesn't outshine my message. But it was a hard one for me to tone things down because I love bright colors, and I love dresses, and I love patterns, and I love bling, and so I was doing all of that, colors and patterns and bling. But people weren't getting to know me for me, they were getting to know me for my clothes and fashion choices. When I go to speak on stage now, I actually remove most of my jewellery. I wear simple earrings. I don't wear noisy bracelets, and I choose a plain dress. I still wear bright colors, because that's me and how I feel most comfortable. I just tone it down a little bit, because I don't want my clothes to outshine my message. I don't want, "Did you see that dress she was wearing? to be the first thing audience members say to each other after hearing me speak. I don't want the first impression of me to be, "she owns a beautiful necklace." This was the right choice for me because I'm a public figure and so I want them to be curious about me, not my appearance. And I want the same thing for you. Be visible in how you dress. If you like to sport lots of makeup and wear loud clothes with bright colors and crazy patterns, go for it. Just make sure your look is appropriate and in sync with you and your goals. Make sure what you wear portrays the message you want to spread.

2. Celebrate!

Celebrating is the second way you can shine brighter. To be clear, I'm encouraging you to celebrate, not brag. I know many women struggle with bragging, and bragging should always be avoided. But you should celebrate your successes. Share that with others. Highlight the good in your life. When someone says, "How's it going?" don't merely say, "fine." Say, "Great, this just happened in my life."

"Great, I'm running this amazing program with over twenty women and I'm really enjoying it."

"Great, I just hung out with my friend this morning and she and I, we have such a strong relationship."

I don't need to go into all the details of The Secret and the Law of Attraction, but I want you to understand how those principles are relevant to this Pillar. When you are celebrating, you are, in that moment, building momentum for the future. As you celebrate success, you are, in that very moment, amplifying your motivation to do more in order to succeed more in the future. Celebrating draws the right kind of energy towards you. When you share the good things that are happening in your life with others, you emit positive vibes, attracting more good things to come. People enjoy talking to people who celebrate. Because it's so much nicer to talk to somebody regarding that great friend she just hung out with, rather than the fight she had with her kid that morning.

I am not saying you can't be real. I'm not telling you to always be celebrating, even in the face of tragedy and disappointment. In fact, I encourage you to reach out to others when you need support. If you need to, I encourage you to talk about your struggles and misfortune. But how you talk about them is important. Don't start off with a 'Negative Nancy' comment or story. Don't immediately conversationally dive into an unfortunate experience you've had. Share something positive, and then as the conversation goes on, if you want to be more vulnerable and share something regarding obstacles or challenges, that's okay. But always begin and end with something positive. Emphasizing the good is important.

If you struggle with celebrating and sharing your reasons for celebrating, talk about the great activities and people with whom you are involved. Eventually, celebrating will come easier as you watch other people celebrate with you. You don't need to say, "I am so awesome. I did this program and everybody loves me." We're definitely not doing that. We don't want our egos to take us over and turn our magnetic confidence into repelling arrogance. But to say, "I'm so proud of these wonderful ladies I'm working with, who are making great changes in their lives and are becoming even more dynamic." Other people will be able to share in that kind of celebration with you. They will be engaged in that kind of positivity, soaking it up and you with it.

3. Speak Your Heart

I was thinking of naming this one "share your dreams," but I think sharing your dreams is only part of speaking your heart. When you share what's truly in your heart, what's close to you, what's important to you and why, you light up. I'm not a fan of doing my taxes so I pass it off to the experts, so if someone asked me to talk about taxes, well, you can imagine the tone in my voice. You can visualize the lack of positive energy in my facial expressions. But if you ask me to tell you about my son riding his bike or my daughter telling jokes, my face is going to light up. You can literally see the difference. When you speak your heart, you talk about what is important to you, and when you do, your whole being changes. The depth of sharing changes. You talk about your dreams. You talk about your passions. You talk about your purpose. You talk about these things from your heart. Instead of sharing obstacles, you share opportunities. You say, "I have an opportunity to grow here, in this way." You never know what's going to happen.

I was recently chatting with someone regarding how my closet was full of professional dresses, but not a lot of cocktail dresses. And after losing forty pounds, most of those dresses didn't fit me anymore anyway. I shared that I would be attending a big, fancy event hosted by a client of mine. I was asked if I would speak from stage at the event—and so I needed just the right outfit for the occasion. But I didn't have much time to find it. I couldn't hit a store, and so I reached out to my friends and told them I needed to borrow something so that I could shine at my client's event. One friend of mine stepped up and said, "Yes, come and shop my closet." I ended up borrowing a beautiful red dress from her for the event.

While wearing that dress at the event, a lady who I didn't know very well (but wanted to) complimented my dress. I told her, "Thank you," and shared how grateful I was for the relationship I had with the friend who lent it to me. I told her the funny story of my picking the dress up from her house, and that my friend said to me, "Oh, my gosh, can I have a shower since you're here?" She went off and showered and I took care of her kids, and we joked about that being my rental payment for the dress. In sharing this and talking about my friend, this woman learned about me and came to understand my values. She probably saw how I value my relationships, how my friends are willing to step up and help me out. But she also saw that I help my friends too when they need me. She learned a lot about me, and I ended up shining in that story. But not because I was bragging about myself, but because I was speaking from my heart about things that are important to me.

When you share your successes, which is important because you need to celebrate them, it inspires others. And when you talk and share from your heart, people get to know you on the inside—your priorities and your values.

The coolest part of this story was when the lady asked me, "You need some party dresses, some cocktail dresses?" To which I replied, "Yes, I do." And then she said, "I'll tell you about this special sale that's happening soon, and you can come with me, and then you can get some more party dresses." I felt incredibly special because you could only attend this sale by invitation only, as it was reserved for the friends and family of this woman. Because I shared from my heart, she then shared with me and invited me to this great sale. I'll tell you what though, I got some great dresses and more at her private sale event!

When you speak from your heart, people will see the inside of you, and your valuable inside will shine outwards. I want to ask you though, after reading the last two ways to shine, i.e., sharing your successes and sharing from the heart, do you need to practice one or more of these? Which one is it? Are you good at sharing your successes? Are you good at sharing from your heart? Are you terrible at both? Are you an expert at both? Let's share that on the Facebook page. Share which one is easy for you, and if neither of them are easy, share that too. Because I want to support you in discovering ways to make sure that you shine.

4. Up Level

So far we've discussed being visible, celebrating, and sharing from your heart. This next one is called levelling up. Up level! This is so important. If we think of the diamond, over time what needs to happen to it? It needs a little bit of sparkle, and so we shine it. If we don't take care of our diamonds, they become dull. Likewise, we become dull by staying the same, by neglecting ourselves. But by creating some friction, you can make yourself shine. Remember this metaphor anytime you face an obstacle or you hit a learning curve. If we keep growing, if we keep placing ourselves in situations that help us grow, if we keep pursuing new experiences with new people who will move us forward, that's how we level up.

When it comes to shining, you need to make sure you are shining in the right place. Do you find yourself to be the big fish in your own little pond? Maybe you feel like, "I'm big in my pond, my shining is so big. I shine so much." Great, it might be that nobody else is shining very brightly, and so you can easily outshine everyone else in your pond. But when you're shining becomes too bright for your environment, you want to find another pond, and then go and start shining in that pond. I challenge you to up level. Up level in your life by being around other people who shine, placing yourself in situations where people are shining, and start to shine your light there too. I want you to be thinking about this beam of light coming out of you, and the strength of your glow. You want to be glowing. You want to be pushing this out, and if you're doing it in such a small place, you're not going to impact others with your purpose and your passions. Up levelling is part of shining.

5. Say Yes to Opportunities

The last one, the fifth one, is to say yes to your own opportunities as well as others. Let's discuss both. You want to shine for your own reasons. If you have written a book, you can stand in that success. You can say, "This is my book." Shine because you are leading something, or shine because you are hosting an event. Shine because you did a great job on your project, that's important because it shows what you're doing in your life path. Shine for your own opportunities, and then shine for others.

The client I mentioned earlier who had that big event, I made sure she was shining. I made sure she was shining not only at the end of the event, but during it and for weeks to come. And because I was supporting her, I got to shine as her coach. I never stole her spotlight, but in a way, her successes became my own. Even though I mention supporting others as a way to shine, you don't want to only shine because of the success of others. You want to shine for your own successes as well. When you're the one shining, it's like the spotlight is on you. And when you're helping others shine, it's as though a whole set of lights are shining and one of the rays lands on you. Picture the difference between one big light and many different, smaller lights. With the many smaller lights, rays radiate from all different directions. And when your light shines for your things, it will move you forward more powerfully along your path, building your legacy along the way. That's what we want to do. We shine for the purpose of living a more fulfilling life, and obviously, being a more Dynamic Woman™ is how we get there.

These are the five ways you can shine more in your life:

1. Be visible
2. Celebrate
3. Speak your heart
4. Up level, and
5. Say Yes to Opportunities.

Here are some suggestions for you to share on the Dynamic You™ Global Community:

- In which of the six levels do you shine? For example, are you being seen or are you invisible?
- Is it easier to share your successes and celebrate? Or is it easier for you to share from your heart?

Here is Your Challenge

Are you ready? The final challenge is to shine strong. I have created a Dynamic You™ Celebration Survey for you to fill out. You'll find as a file on the Dynamic You™ Global Community Page on Facebook. You can also find the questions from it are in the next Chapter. In the Dynamic You™ Celebration Survey you're going to write down your successes. Your challenge is to then share your successes online. How does that feel? Scary? I would love to see you shine. I would love to see you shining on video. You can prerecord it if you want, or you can do a live video, whatever you want to do. But I want you to talk about how over the course of the book, you've changed. How you have stepped into your Dynamic You™. I want you to highlight all the amazing things that have happened to you and what you have accomplished.

Why?

- For the purpose of shining.
- You are going to be visible.
- You are celebrating your success.
- You are going to be speaking from your heart.
- You are going to be up levelling yourself because you are saying yes to an opportunity.

What's the opportunity? When you share this, tag me so I see it @LifeCoachDiane and use the hashtags:

#DynamicYouBook, #IamDynamic and #DynamicWomen

Also, when you tag me, it's going to be on my feed as well. This is an amazing opportunity for you to shine as one of my people to my people. There can be some good opportunities for you. I know that as you share from your heart and share your successes, you're going to inspire others. You're going to motivate others. That's what Dynamic Women™ do, right? We step up and we come to this place where others grow because of us. And who knows? Someone on my list could be looking for someone like you.

You can do it! And after you share, you'll be rewarded. What I'm going to do is offer you a Dynamic You™ Celebration Session ($350 Value)! We will speak over the phone, and I'll help you celebrate you and your growth. We will lock in all that you have learned, and I'll help you figure out what the next steps should be. The ladies who have had this session have been so grateful for that one-on-one time together, and to get a plan in place. So get those videos up and tag me! I can't wait to watch them!

How Was The Challenge?

Tazeem Jamal, "As social as I am on the outside & I LOVE to meet new people, I can get 'paralyzed' sometimes when I am out! I find I have to use positive self-talk when I'm going into social situations. If I am 'working' an event or involved, then it's easier to connect with others, I'm not really sure why.

"I believe I show up 'being Witnessed' 85% of the time. I use 'dressing for success' as a way to boost my confidence. I for sure use on & offline to maintain my 'presence,' and I challenge myself to UP LEVEL and love to surround myself with people that push their own boundaries! That's inspiring to me {another reason I LOVE this group!} Feel the fear & do it anyway!

"I LOVE to connect with others, give them KUDOS & congratulate them on things going on in their lives, but when the tables are flipped & it's time for me to SHINE, I can feel a little overwhelmed & want to deflect it! I'm learning every day to embrace all this POSITIVE energy, as it does fuel me, I just have to honor when others GIFT me kind & generous words.

"I strive to be a better version of myself everyday & being around all of you in the program, the safety & love of this group is incredible! I love how we don't judge each other, but reach out from a place of authentic support! Thank you to Diane Rolston Coaching & all of you for that!

"When I first met Diane, I had been through a really difficult time in my life & needed to be surrounded by supportive & kind women! I have grown so much & the journey continues! The biggest gift for me has been allowing myself to feel vulnerable & sharing. Asking for help was really really hard, but now I feel like I can ask!"

Claudine Pender, "How do I show up? I try hard to BLEND IN because I was told I speak too much, laugh too much, am too loud, etc. But I FEEL most of the time I am being SEEN, I am WITNESSED about 40-50% of the time. I SHINE at a level six, only when I am totally comfortable, and I would say that's 5-10% of the time. Nobody does that to me. I do it all to myself!

"When I look at the ways to increase my ability to shine, I have a few thoughts on each one:

"1. Be visible! I try to blend in, so I'm not bold in my clothes. I have been told I try to hide myself, actually (with my clothes). I also really love black/white and gray! I AM where my people are! I LOVE being part of my community, and as you can see, I do my best to be active, supportive, and KIND. I avoid "showing off" so I might have missed opportunities to do videos, etc. I will work on that! I don't want to BOTHER people, so perhaps I am not as visible just not to bother people.

"2. Celebrate! I share my successes. I just don't do it enough, I guess. I am positive, I am good at that!

"3. Speak your heart! I do that!

"4. Up level! I DON'T do that—yet.

"5. Say YES to opportunities! I feel I SHINE more for others than for myself. But I do speak about my successes lately. Something to work more on! I will figure out how to do the video and share it."

Anneliese Dusseldorp, "This has been a tough Pillar. Good though, as I aspire to be a shining dynamic woman. I actually shed a tear while I learned about the Pillar. I feel like I am a level 6 when I attend Dynamic Women™ events and Send Out Cards events, but when I am at networking events or a my day job, I am at a level 3 or 4."

Cora Naylor, "I fluctuate between all the levels. My goal is to be a 5/6, but sometimes in certain situations, especially large gatherings where I don't know people, I can revert to a 2/3. When I'm not feeling my best, I tend to want to be a 1, but know that it's not a good place to be, so I don't stay there long. I am definitely doing this to myself. "I find it much easier to share from the heart than to celebrate something else I am working on."

Angela Foran, "For the most part, I would say I fluctuate between levels 4-6, depending on the situation, my mood, and the people I'm with. I tend to slip into level 3 when I'm at a large event that is outside of my field. I like to get a feel for the people and the energy of the event so I can purposely blend in. Every so often, I go into hiding, usually more to recharge than to avoid shining. I don't have a lot of stamina for big events. I can be at a level 5 or 6 if I am around my people, but if I'm not then, I will dip down to a 2 or 3. I feel like I should be more visible, but actually don't have the desire to be.

"I am much better at speaking my heart than celebrating. I find that when I do reach my goals, I don't celebrate because I am always looking ahead to what is next. I think that is why it's hard for me to really see what I have accomplished because I have never taken the time to look back. I think last year was the first time I reviewed my year and actually wrote down goals. Despite not writing goals, I am always up leveling: taking courses, taking on different jobs, workshops, pretty much whatever comes my way. Which I guess goes with saying yes to opportunities. I always say yes because I really enjoy doing new things."

Then I asked *Angela*, "I'm curious about this sentence, *Angela:* 'I feel like I should be more visible, but actually don't have the desire to be.' What's 'the should be' about? In service of what? And you don't desire to be visible, then what do you desire to be?"

Angela replied, "I thought the should might catch your attention, you have called me on that before. I think when I hear the word visible, it means joining different clubs/committees, attending lots of events, volunteering, etc. And so when I say I feel like I should be more visible, I think that is my real or imagined feeling of other people's judgment or expectation that this is what I 'should' be doing as a business owner. Does that make sense? So in this way, I want to hide, see patients, tinker away in my apothecary, stay home or read a book. I think being visible takes a lot of energy for me, partially because of issues with Pillar 8 and my indecisiveness. What do I desire to be? I'll have to think about that."

Pam Karlen, "I definitely am shining brighter after the Dynamic You™ program and one-on-one coaching with Diane Rolston Coaching for 6 months.

"I have been at all the levels, [and] I now have great awareness to see where I have been. Right now I would say I am getting into Witness mode, so I need to keep working so I can get to SHINE level. Whoop! I'm celebrating how far I have come! Complete participation in the Dynamic You™ program is another whoop! It feels good to totally complete a commitment."

Chantal Staaf, "Good evening everyone! Over the last few weeks I have been learning to love myself the way I am; the good and the faults. Acknowledging my strengths, my awesomeness and where I need to focus my energy. Today I was grateful to have met an insightful woman with a message, 'Stop not giving your full self.'

"This is my first step. I carry much guilt and denial around the fact I have. This is not something I share, as I had been choosing to live in denial. But how can I grow and love and embrace who I am if I am in denial of this big part of my life? Despite the fact I'm not going to stand on rooftops and share, [I] thought this would be a great start."

Fatima Sumar, "Wow, I have not done Pillar Eight, but based on the comments that I have read, this is going to be big Pillar for me. At different junctions, I am guilty of using all seven killers and resonated with each one. Growing up, I was never good enough, and was always compared to everyone else. I was either too fat, too shy because I would be judged for everything I said, I was not smart enough, I would not succeed, I was not too conniving enough, I was too emotional or sensitive, I'm too nice of a person to get ahead in life... and the list continues. Over the past six years I have been working hard to reverse that. I know that I'm me and I'm perfect the way I am in my head, but [I] sometimes lack that feeling in my heart, and that is when I spiral into a war path of self-pity."

"This challenge was rather tough. I went live the first time and deleted it, then started going on Instagram to waste time. It turns out, I was afraid of what people would say.

"It's funny, how I had so much in my mind to say but could not say the stuff, rather just went with the flow. Another thing, I tend to overthink and improve. Thank you ladies for being a part of this journey of mine, and Thank you Diane Rolston Coaching for sparking the inner conversations for us to shine."

Claudine Pender, "I just went through the final part of Dynamic You™, and I had tears in my eyes at the beginning when you asked, "how do you feel?" and at the end I felt, "I don't want this to end!!!"I feel I have grown a lot! I not only loved this program, I also love our group. I didn't imagine it would be this powerful. You really are amazing and you attract the same kind of people, Diane Rolston Coaching."

Fatima Sumar, "I had an interesting and insightful experience over the past couple of days. Where in one of my volunteer positions, I had asked my lead for a roles and responsibilities outline, and she was the only one that could complete it, as it was for her role. She was given over a week to complete it, and when I sent her a gentle reminder, she gave in her formal resignation.

"I was fuming and walked away from my phone to avoid a nasty email. I called up a girlfriend, who is one of my 5 that I will bounce ideas off for a perspective change. Anyways, what she was saying was not sitting well with me. I then put everything aside and told my saboteur to go take a long hike up the Chief and the Grouse Grind (two big hikes in Vancouver and Squamish) so I could focus on other important matters.

"As I was driving, I realized that she needed her space to cool off, and if I had sent her any email at that point, it would create a sour impression and I still have to work with her in other areas. Two days later, I finally responded, gracefully accepting her resignation and wishing her all the best in her commitments and future endeavors. It felt good to be Dynamic and take my time to respond."

Sukeina Jethabhai, "I think one of my most important lessons this week is that there is no judgment in self-awareness. It's important to realize who you are, and then accept and move forward from there, no need to beat yourself up. I also realized that I want to increase my connectivity to other women in the professional world and build a deeper connection with them. This week, I was lucky to find a coworker who has a good connection with She Talks, and I reached out to her to see if she could help me join the organizing team. Crossing my fingers that some good comes of it, and if not, I'll keep trying to move forward in other ways."

Cora Naylor, "Got to practice Pillars 4 & 5 today. Was out and about doing errands and meetings today, and it seemed like every time I was distracted from what I was doing, something would get in my way, for example, waiting for the train or someone late for an appointment. Each time I changed my perspective. I could have been upset, but instead [I] chose to think that the universe is telling me to slow down and 'smell the roses,' so each time I took a few good breaths and enjoyed my surroundings. I'm happy to say it ended up being a great day!"

CHAPTER 11
YOUR NEXT STEPS

And here we are, at the end. I feel like I should give some high fives! But since you are there and I'm here, please put your right hand on your back and pat it at least 10 times. Then place your right hand on your heart and cover it with the left. Take a moment to connect with yourself.

- You have mattered enough to read this book.
- You have created time and space for yourself.
- You made yourself a priority.
- You brought each of the nine Pillars into your life.

Feel the shift that's happened.

Unleash Your Dynamic Woman™

You now have the secret code of Dynamic Women™ who are confident, wealthy and successful! Have you unleashed the Dynamic Woman™ in you yet? She is either out now or working her way out. So as a percentage how much is she out? 10%? 50%? 100%

Whatever the number, your journey doesn't stop here. Now that you know the nine Pillars, the next step is to implement them, live them, and BE THEM! Right now, make a quarterly date with yourself in your calendar to review the Pillars, to review your notes, and to take on the challenges that you need.

Dynamic You™ Celebration Survey

1. Looking at each Pillar, give yourself a score from 1 – 10 for how much you were living in that Pillar before and after the program. 10 is fully living in it all the time and 1 is not at all.

Pillar	Before	After
1. Prioritized		
2. Real		
3. Connected		
4. Perspective		
5. Self-Aware		
6. Magnetic		
7. Collaboration		
8. Confident		
9. Shining		

3. Recall where you were when the coaching began. Compare that version of yourself to where you are now. What achievements (internal and external) would you like to celebrate?

4. What gifts have you gained from this journey that will support you into the future?

4. Where have you grown the most?

5. What changes are you committed to keeping?

6. Are there things that remain unresolved? What do you need to do? What does your soul desire?

7. What were some of your most important discoveries? What tools and techniques do you now have?

8. According to what you learned, how have you unleashed the DYNAMIC woman in YOU?

Have You Done Your Pillar 9 Challenge?

Below are video transcriptions from some of the ladies in the six-week program.

Sandra Girard, "As they say, all good things must come to an end, and I've really enjoyed our time together in doing this program with Diane and others in the Dynamic You™ Program. I have to admit, it wasn't easy. It was challenging at times—the time commitment, making sure I invested that time into myself, scheduled that time, and also it made me stretch in ways that maybe I wasn't so comfortable with.

"But what I have learned just reconfirms that I am dynamic. And there are many things that I can celebrate with, and many areas that I shine and I sparkle. Those are things that I really pay attention to. What are the things that make me sparkle, and be authentic, and be me and celebrate me? And I'm going to start paying more attention to those things and those people that make me feel that way. I've been saying for a while that I've been looking for a new sandbox, and to think that you ladies are a part of my new sandbox, and it just makes me happy to know that I'm going to continue to grow and stretch and be surrounded by like-minded women.

"For that, I'm thankful. Thank you to all of you for that. It's not the end, it's the beginning of new things for all of us that we can celebrate and congratulate each other on. I look forward to having our paths cross again and getting involved in many other ways with each other and through this program. Thank you again, Diane. You are dynamic, and thank you for sharing your knowledge and your passion with us. Thank you."

Chantal Staaf, "I want to mention I'm thankful that I met—well I haven't met Diane in real life—but I'm really thankful that I got included in this group. That was a big step for me, committing the money, the time, more so the time for me and some personal growth. Thank you for that. I think the biggest thing that I learned was just that taking a bit more time for myself and being secure in my decisions, that's been tested very recently quite a few times in different parts of my life. And despite the fact that sometimes they're not the right decisions, they are the decisions that I made and that's what it is. I think, without this program, I would be second-guessing myself a lot more than I am. Thank you to everyone, thank you Diane, and we'll be in touch."

Sukeina Jethabhai, "I'm finally doing this video. It's been a long time coming, I know I'm delayed; I'm still working on that P in procrastination for those self-confidence killers.

"First and foremost, I just wanted to let everybody know that I haven't heard anybody's videos yet, and I did that intentionally because I was afraid of compare-itis. I wanted you to know that it's been an amazing six weeks that we've had together, and I've seen some strong changes in myself.

"Some of the things that I felt coming out of the Dynamic You™ Program were that I started to really believe in myself and own who I am and that has been huge for me. Being able to do that has deterred me less when I get feedback or comments that are maybe off-hand, either negative or positive, it doesn't bother me as much and doesn't elate me as much because I am more grounded in who I am.

"The other thing is I finally leapt into my fear, and last week, Friday, I handed in my resignation. By the end of January, I will have stopped working at a company that I've been at for the last nine and a half years. I love the company, I love the role, and I love, of course, the income that I was getting from it. However, I knew I had outgrown the role and the company and it was time for me to move on.

"I thought, you know what, I'm going to leap into my fear. I've got a window of about a year where I can handle being a one-income home—where we could do this as a family. I'm hoping to get myself organized so that when I do leave my job at the end of January, I can either leap into a side business or do other things that have been on my bucket list and really face those fears and grow in new ways. I don't think I could've done it so soon if I hadn't done the Dynamic You™ Program. Thank you Diane for helping me develop that courage over the last six weeks."

What Do You Want To Share?

I know you've done well and lots of shifts have taken place, so share them with me. Share the answers to the questions above, tell me your story, or share how this book has helped you unleash your Dynamic You™. You know, I'm actually fuelled by knowing I have made a difference in your life. AND then I get to celebrate you!

My Final Thoughts And A Gift

It's been my joy to deliver these nine Pillars to you. Thank you so much for trusting me to take you along this journey. However, no journey is ever complete, and I know you have more you want to accomplish. So I have a gift for you, so you can continue to build on the success you have already had.

Go to this address below. It is private for only women like you who have read the book. You will find gifts from me, extra resources, videos and more. And I will keep adding to it, updating it, and sharing more of my findings and teachings.

www.dianerolston.com/dynamicyougift

One last thing I'd like to share with you...

I imagine a world where all women
love themselves for who they are.
Where they stop being their own worst critic
and instead celebrate their progress.
Women who fall fast
and get up just as quick.
Who make themselves a priority.
Who live their legacy.
Who speak up.
You are this woman!
A Dynamic Woman!
Congrats!

Stay Dynamic!

DYNAMIC YOU™ PROGRAM PARTICIPANTS

Here are just a few of the many Dynamic Women™ who have graciously shared their experiences in going through the Nine Pillars during the six-week Live Dynamic You™ Program.

Melody Owen

Founder of Nutritious Truth Publishing
Author, Educator, Mentor

Melody writes books for women who want to change the world by changing themselves. She works with other women ready to tell their unique story to the world in a manner that empowers both the writer and the reader. We all have a story to tell and experiences to share that can enrich the lives of other women. What is your story? Melody has taught writing on three continents, coached communications skills to executives, and worked in publishing in sales, marketing and public relations. She holds a degree from the University of Waterloo in Ontario, Canada.

Claire Madin

Founder & CEO of West Women Trekkers Inc.
Certified Personal Trainer

Claire has an adventurous spirit with a notable Australian accent! Claire is Founder of West Women Trekkers Inc. and is a passionate advocate for women's fitness. In 2016, Claire stepped away from the 9-5 role, strapped on the hiking boots, and started her own company—what an adventure! As a certified personal trainer, Claire encourages women to self-prioritize, and trek train with friends in nature. Most days, Claire can be found (and heard) on the beautiful trails leading, motivating and cheering for her clients as they complete trek training challenges on Vancouver trails.

Cora Naylor

Sapphire Executive – Jeunesse Global
Accountability Coach

Shyness can be overcome, with incentive. For Cora, it was finding Jeunesse, with its supportive team to encourage me while she does the same for others. Throughout her life, she felt like she was sitting on the outside, looking in. she never took control of her own direction. Because of Jeunesse, she has embraced opening up and exploring her personal development to find her passion— which led to her starting an additional business as an Accountability Coach. She loves being an example of the great things that come when you listen to that voice telling you to embrace your fear and reach for what you want.

Chantal Staaf

Senior Leader with Epicure

Chantal lives in Chilliwack, British Columbia. She is wife and a mother of a 15-year-old competitive 'cheerleader' and an 11-year-old competitive dancer and so life is never dull! Chantal has been self-employed for 14 years with Epicure; a direct sales company that demonstrate that healthy cooking doesn't have to be long OR expensive. She has earned trips and has had a lot of great growth and success with the company.

Anneliese Dusseldorp

Senior Manager, SendOutCards

Anneliese is a mother, sister, daughter, and a wife! For the past 13 years, she has always had a deep desire to have her own business, however she was unsure of where to even start. She did lots of research and was actively looking, however, she never really found a company that was was the right fit—until she was introduced to SendOutCards. Since she successfully launched her own SendOutCards business in 2010, she has had the ability to strengthen relationships with her family and friends, made some incredible new friendships, had the chance to travel and help others successfully get started with SendOutCards too!

Tazeem Jamal PMDT, LE

Licensed Esthetician, Spa Business Coach, Allysian Sciences Brand Ambassador

Growing up with globetrotting entrepreneurial parents, Tazeem mastered the art of client care at a very early age. Business was instinctive for Tazeem, and at 21 she embarked on her career as a Clinical Esthetician with Skindulgence Spa. As an award winning business owner and Spa Business Coach, Tazeem is passionate about helping her clients create "The Purple Carpet Experience" in order to stand apart from the crowd. She insightfully assists her clients to think outside of the box, and she shows them how to leverage their time to increase their bottom line with retail sales and marketing.

Sandra Girard

Consultant, Rodan + Fields

Sandra prides herself on her relationships, professionally and personally. Married for 30 years , raised two amazing daughters who continue to inspire her to have fun and dream bigger. In this next chapter of her life, Sandra wants to continue to grow and inspire other women to be their best self and stretch a little. I have been asked to represent many skincare lines over the years and until now, none of them made sense. What I love about Rodan + Fields, is it's not only life changing skincare but it allows me to build a future with my daughters, create time freedom and inspire other women to dream bigger for themselves.

Fatima Sumar

Founder of FireFox Media, Published Poet
Founder of Designs by Fatima Sumar

Fatima is a very creative and passionate woman who strives to make life better for those she works with. Her vibrant energy is contagious and she will always have your back and give you the honest truth whether it comes to your social media marketing or your fashion sense. Fatima is a Dynamic Woman™ with great inner strength and powerful drive to have an incredible life.

Pam Karlen

Certified Coach

As a Certified Coach, Pam Karlen loves connecting with women and sharing how a life change from a professional photographer to life coaching taught her how to let go of what no longer served her and how spiritual connection, mindset and taking intentional action is essential in following your life purpose. "I know when women start feeling good on the inside, amazing things start happening on the outside." Pam works with women who are overwhelmed and frustrated to pause and unlock the greatness that resides inside of them so they can live life full of energy, time and financial freedom.

Sukeina Jethabhai

Senior Project Manager, Press Reader

Sukeina is an experienced Project Manager with a background in computer science, business development and digital marketing. She has worked in the Digital Publishing industry for the past ten years. She has been recognized by her colleagues as someone who can merge the non-technical with the technical to get the job done well. Outside of work, Sukeina is a mother of three teenagers and an active community volunteer who organizes spiritual camps and retreats for both youth and adults. She is an avid learner and a self-development junkie. In 2016, Sukeina took a leap of faith and resigned from her role as a Senior Project Manager to take a year off and build an empire - a tribe as she focuses on the intersection of interior design and inner peace. Her goal is to develop her interior design business and to help others find peace through spirituality, Islamic principles and their environment.

Claudine Pender

Connector, Property Investor

Born in Brazil, Claudine immigrated to Canada in her late 20's with her son and husband in 1995. She has a Bachelor Degree in Public Relations from Brazil and a certificate in Marketing Management from BCIT. After many years working in communication and marketing, she was laid off from a job she really liked, which led her to think she should plan less and go with the flow more. So, as a result of her "letting go of control", her business was born. Amazing circumstances and people led her to a path of starting her own business as a treasure-hunter, furniture painter and eventually shop owner of new and vintage of home décor. Combining the skills and knowledge she learnt through her business and other business people she met along the way, she decided that she wanted to be a property investor. She now rents her properties as vacation suites. She now loves furnishing the spaces with new and vintage items managing the properties and dealing with the guests.

Michelle Abraham

Online Marketing & Business Strategist
Owner of Create Launch Market You

Michelle is a Dynamic Women™, world traveler, adventure seeker, Wife and a busy Mom of two little ones under four years old. She loves being a mom and a savvy business woman and feels much more confident in handling it all with grace and going after her dreams after going through Dynamic You™. Michelle currently spends her time speaking to & consulting professional business owners on technology and online marketing strategy. Michelle's specialty is helping these professionals launch their businesses online to leverage their time and maximize their profits. Michelle helps clients program, package and position themselves as Experts through online courses, social media, podcasting, publishing books and content syndication.

ACKNOWLEDGMENTS

I want to thank my Mother who had an endless belief in me even when I didn't and gave selflessly to our family. To my Father whose hard work and creativity still astound me. To my mentors and coaches along the way, Sonia, Signy and Pamela: who embraced my potential then invited my brilliance out and expanded me from one level to the next.

To those who were part of the journey: my clients who showed up in their mess and their success and inspired this book, my Dynamic Women™ in Action Members who believed in deeper connections and inspired a deeper movement in me and to those ladies who went through Dynamic You™ and breathed life into my concepts.

To those who personally touched the words of this book, my Copy Editor Kaylie, my Stylistic editor Melody and my technical guru Michelle. And everyone who was there with me along the way: Kim who showed me my bigger path, and Tazeem and Rozz for being the ultimate cheerleaders.

To my husband Adriel who never questions my dreams, my kids who help me play and be present and to God for blessing me with my gifts and a huge destiny to fill.

ABOUT THE AUTHOR

Diane Rolston is a leading authority in being a Dynamic Woman and living a Dynamic Life. Combining a mix of coaching and personal development, Diane works with professional women to provide clarity, boost confidence and get them into action. She is a Certified Professional Coach, an engaging speaker, a workshop leader and the CEO of Dynamic Women™ in Action (DWA) a quickly expanding community of women. She received the Vancouver Top Mom Blogger Award in 2016 and was acknowledged as a finalist for the  2014 Leading Mom Award for her professional accomplishments and for the powerful impact she has on the women she inspires and empowers.

Diane left the life of the 9-5 employee and simultaneously became an entrepreneur and mother. Now a mother of two, business owner and community leader she considers herself an expert in change, work/life balance, prioritizing and getting things done! Diane's diverse work experience enables her to have a deeper understanding of what it takes to achieve our best and live with more confidence and satisfaction. She brings this understanding to her role as a workshop leader in her series of programs starting with Dynamic Balance™.

 Diane has presented internationally at women's business seminars, professional development conferences and on telesummits. With clients across North America she has worked with non-profit executives, top management leaders, small business owners, and professional women helping them get better results in a shorter amount of time. She sees women sabotage themselves, get overwhelmed and second-guess their choices and uses her powerful questions to give clarity to what they really want and how they are going to achieve it. In 1:1 coaching sessions or in one of her programs like Dynamic Year™, Dynamic Power™ and the She's Goaled™

Coaching Mastermind Program, she helps people break down big goals and build confidence so they can tackle their greatest obstacles and fears towards their success.

With her special mix of dynamics and heart she founded the group called, Dynamic Women™ in Action, where she facilitates engaging activities to help women get clearer about their greatness, success catalysts and the solutions to the obstacles (and all the while building strong relationships with other dynamic women). In only a few years the DWA™ community has grown to over 700 women and expanded to multiple locations.

Clients tell Diane that they love her sense of humor. That, "She's a positive person who constantly challenges your limits and helps you keep growing". And she's known for cracking a joke as easily as she cracks the whip! Audiences comment on her dynamic style and how she always gives them a tool or challenge they can put into action and inspires them to make the changes they have been putting off.

In her own pursuits she pushes her limits, faces what scares her and never passes up a great dessert. As a mother, wife, coach and business owner Diane acts with love and courage because she knows that in all parts of our life, we have the opportunity to inspire others. More than anything, she focuses on her goals in life and helps other women do the same.

To work with Diane 1:1 or in a Group Program

please go to www.DianeRolston.com

and request a chat to see if you're a fit.

To book Diane to speak at your event

please email her at diane@dianerolston.com.

Made in the USA
Middletown, DE
14 April 2017